WARS
OF THE
MIND

VOLUME 4:
(*On-Top a Hill – Beneath a Tall Tree.*)

By: Jonathan *W.* Haubert

Edited By: Jonathan W. Haubert

8	X	8

Order this book online at www.trafford.com
or email orders@trafford.com

Most Trafford titles are also available at major online book retailers.

Printed in the United States of America.

ISBN: 978-1-4907-2179-8 (sc)
ISBN: 978-1-4907-2178-1 (e)

Library of Congress Control Number: 2013922880

Trafford rev. 03/13/2014

 www.trafford.com

North America & international
toll-free: 1 888 232 4444 (USA & Canada)
fax: 812 355 4082

"Fuck..."

Wars of the Mind Contents:

Chapter 4 – *Finders Keepers.*

Chapter 13 – *On-top a Hill - Beneath a Tall Tree*

Chapter 1

One Step Further - Beyond Another Step.

Proud

One step further, beyond another step.
Two steps taken, beyond all the rest.
One lie told, for no true reason at all.
So take my hand and laugh, as we both begin to fall...

Into the deepest part, of what they say is real.
Then we shelter ourselves in darkness, hoping these wounds will heal.
But it really doesn't matter, to no one but you and I.
So I am proud to be here now, proud to say that I'm alive.

Shit

Cold - as the rotting carcass of the child lies awake in the womb.
Dreaming and hoping he may someday reach the tomb.
It withers - the thought of when you held me so close.
Nothing truly remains now, say for this sad and lonely ghost.

Twisted – as all of their faces press through the screen.
I pinch myself and draw blood, because it might just be a dream.
But no matter how hard we try to say, that it's all going to be okay.
We have to come to terms with inevitability and *get ready for our graves.*

Cold – as the rotting carcass of the child lies awake in the womb.
Feeling the burn as *Mother* and *God* bring forth our doom.
So I begin to realize the truth that I just never could get.
Is that all I ever meant to you, was nothing more than shit...

Madness-Joy

Pages fluttering inside my brain, a growing tornado I like to call rage.
The stones they throw, are the only ground on which for us to step.
The glass might have been half full, but they all took a sip.
Now passion is the only thing that binds me to humanity.
But then again, the true joke was *the lie called sanity...*
Pages fluttering inside my veins, pumping reality into the grave.
For any other reason, we need not give them today.
So now the glass is empty, nothing more than a stain.
Then the voices speak up but no one's left to hear.
Pages burning inside my hollow heart.
Bring forth the *Madness-Joy* of another year.

Feeble & Frail

Feeble and frail, all day talking to myself and still I get no reply.
The motion sticks, "I guess this is it," so maybe we should close our eyes.
The days seem shorter yet somehow I know the weight of *Time's Sand*.
So I kiss you now upon your heart, but I don't think you understand.

Beaten and brittle, dragging myself one inch closer to the fact.
The drug can't stop me this time, so just try to relax.
And there it sits steaming, the rusted and bloody blade of the ax.
Stuck in that worthless stump called her head.
I pull it out with a jerk, then watch as the blood drains down onto her breast.

Feeble and frail, today I awoke in hell, and still I can't see the light.
The notions pushed, a bleeding sore in the middle of your heart.
The thought of what you've become, it truly tears me apart.
But I know that in this fucked up reality, "I've truly got the upper-hand."

Talking to Myself

Constant voices creeping over my flesh causing chills every time.
The mirror asked me how I was doing, "well I guess I've been fine."
So how far have I come, in this damned eternal rhyme.
It did tickle at first, and now burning needles into my spine…

What have I said to be treated this way, so useless like trash?
How much more will it take, before I can take a glance back?
It seems so wrong, all the stirring voices that now reach the top.
Someone get me out of this shell, but I think the door has been locked.

Nerves now numb faded and dead, as I move onward into the haze.
Although I know that I don't truly exist, still I have a smile on my face.
Just let me see, as the snow falls once more onto her soft lips.
Then I think I could let go, and admit that I am truly sick.

So where am I going, and how long have I been gone?
Is anyone out there, please somebody sing along…
It's not working now, so I guess I'll just shout.
Still I get no answer, because I've only been talking to myself.

Butterflies...

At first I just can't seem to find the words.
She places her hand over my heart and looks into my eyes.
I try my hardest but still no words.
All I can seem to do is watch her stare into my mind.
Nothing seems to surface anymore, only the thought of her smile.
Then I feel them begin to flutter, growing from deep inside.

She takes my hand and guides me away from all my fears.
She says not a thing, but I know she's the one that cares.
I need to speak something, but nothing seems great enough to say.
I can only feel the butterflies, swarming within my brain.
But she doesn't seem to mind, she just guides me on into the light.
I know I'm just a little nervous at first, and had nothing much to say.
But maybe I can smile now, because all the butterflies have flown away.

Okay

Okay then, so what's my fucked up problem today?!
I've done my very best, but for some reason I was still thrown away.
Okay then, let's say that we mean more in the heart of our lord.
Then you come to realize the fact, *that you were only a worthless whore.*

Just a moment please, I need to get a better grip on this blade.
I need another second, then the wind can blow it all away.
Because we had laughed at the sight of the angel's tormented screams.
That is why all along, you "my love" were nothing more than a sad dream...

Okay then, so what the fuck now am I going to say?!
I've done said I tried my best, but who gives a shit anyways?
Okay then, take your hand and reach it far into my brain.
You pull out only the dirt and ash of my grave but don't worry yourself.
It's all going to be okay...

Ever Dead

Growing now, the waking thoughts of the Ever Dead.
Showing now, the troubled breaking notions inside your head.
It's not over now, we still have much more to go.
A damned eternal voyage, through the thirteen oceans of snow.

A bitter pause, because someone close has passed away.
A lingering fog, leaving our once beautiful earth stained.
Now all is lost, or is it us that just cannot be found?
If you truly have the gall, then stand up now and shout!

Growing stronger, the waking thoughts of the Ever Dead.
Slowing down, the Magic Bullet inside your head.
It's not over now, we still must make it to the dawn.
I know you're dead, but please - try to hold on...

Bones Against You...

Can you feel it writhing, a slam and then a hit.
Now you want to hurry and leave, but you won't ever be missed.
So you kissed it all goodbye, when you decided to live a lie.
Now there is nothing much we can say or do.
When all these bones have been pushed against you.

So there's a smile on your face and that notion you can't just erase.
Well get over it then, just let it all go and escape with the wind.
Into a better thought, but now you feel it begin to tear.
Just laugh now while you can, because no one here cares.

Can you feel it writhing, as you try to exhale the tar?
Now the last hope of ever regaining, is hidden beneath the scars.
So what truly now can you say, what is it that you can do.
You can no longer escape because all the bones now grind against you...

"Lost is Alone Am I?"

So now is the time for some new views.
Now is the time for some new faith.
Now it is the time, for you to see the demon's face.
"The mask that could never be..."

Over time and time, then so many lonely and sad drinks.
I ask you to pull the trigger, and try not to blink.
Then let me know what you've seen, "was it something great?"
Now I feel only cold, as I wake up on the same damn page.

They hold over with counterfeit smiles, but I know they're fake.
I try my very best to play along, with their sick demented games.
But now I know, some things in this world *"never really change."*
It is truly pointless now, so please just go away.

For months of trying to be heard, knowing no one's there.
Years of saying that you're sorry, but God doesn't care.
It seems like no one's there, nobody standing at my side.
That's what I get for being to one who tried, so now *lost is alone am I?*

Above the Bottom Lip

She places a razor above the bottom lip.
Then she grins as she commences to giving me a kiss.
In the middle of my throat, I feel a slight choke.
As I look into her eyes, I feel I can no longer breathe.

It was for reasons, we need not say today.
Now I understand, why God told us to look away.
But the fact is, "the blade is more of a pleasure than a pain."
It makes me feel right at home, but most call it insane.

She takes my hand and places it between her legs.
So I grin, that same damn smile of yesterday.
Then she places her tongue, above my bottom lip.
I guess I can only smile, as I give *Death* a kiss.

_Perpetual Agon_y

This desert, why the hell does it feel so cold and jaded?
A million miles to _Nowhere_, and thousands of more hours wasted.
The sand is so hot, yet my body begins to freeze.
Still I drag myself further, if even on my hands and knees.

So what is it I seek, it must be something unable to find.
What is it that I've been longing for, _"now I must be blind?"_
So all the torment, is again infesting my brain.
But the funny part is, it never really went away…

This desert, why is the sand such a dark-red?
Then I begin to realize, that it's all inside my head.
For so many years now, I've sat here beneath the rainy clouds.
Waiting and waiting for this _perpetual agony_ to come to an end…

Spilt Salt

Twisting are the faces that won't let me find any rest.
Locked beneath the pavement, lost inside my own head.
They say that I'm a dreamer, although I never sleep at night.
I think I can hold on a little longer, so it's going to be alright.

They tell me to get my shit straight and stand up for myself.
"I've tried all that, then for a decade I fell."
So what was the purpose, why did I even try?
I only wanted to hold you once more, before you hit the lights.

Can't get a grip and then I feel it start to slip, as I watch it all fall away.
The Devil makes a wish, and then an _Angel_ gives me a kiss.
It feels so strange to watch our whole universe melt away.
I just can't find a grip, so I guess this is it.
The salt is spilt, "we're shit out of luck," and now our damnation begins today.

22

Blood on the Rose

The moon hangs alone in the middle of starless night sky.
So dark now, it's pointless to even try opening your eyes.
I lay in *horror and doubt*, of the fact that God and the Devil knows.
So still I will lie here waiting, for the sun to melt away the snow.

The words seem further, I can't seem to get a grip today.
The moon hangs alone in the sky, slowly erasing yesterday.
And she is hoping tranquility but only because it's dark out.
I lie here alone, still my mind aches with doubt.

Our world is turning, *tilted it spins* cradled in space.
So dark now, "colors faded," food and drink has all lost its taste.
Now I have only the pleasure of the smoke that our God and Devil knows.
And so she sits there all night weeping - *blood on the rose...*

Moons of Saturn

The smile of a child, so innocent it proves there must be hope.
Again for ages we wander, through the endless tome of notes.
"You strive so hard to find something, which might hold a greater clarity."
Now you understand why, there is no hope for humanity.

We drift further now, beyond the reasons of the beast.
We've tried our hardest, but we're still so naïve.
Could we ever be forgiven, for all our accumulated sins?
So we venture now deeper, into the middle of the wrist.

So far out beyond all the screams and pain.
Alone on a bad trip, lying back in an open grave.
And it seems that all that comes to mind is nothing but laughter.
So I guess I'll take *that trip*, far beyond the *Moons of Saturn*.

Angels in the Smoke

Angels dancing in the smoke - The Devil laughing as I choke.
Demons hounding me - For all my sins.
My lungs are about gone now, but we light it up once again.

Angels singing in the smoke - This heart feels numb because it's broke.
The demons loathe me - Yet we are the same.
Their song is so soothing, but with the smoke it fades.

Angels laughing in the smoke - The Devil knows I was nothing but a joke.
The world it hates me - I am just worthless trash.
I know you once loved me, and yet you threw me back.

Angels screaming in the smoke - And I laugh as they all choke.
Demons now respect me - For we are the same.
The angels smile and give to me a *Jagged Kiss*, as now the smoke all fades away.

Feeding My Heart to You…

Are you hungry my dear, please let me fix you something to eat.
So I rip my heart from my chest, and I laugh as slowly it bleeds.
Do you like it sweet, or would you rather have it bitter like you?
I could grill it in the flames of hell, or mixed with tar I'll make a nice stew.

Are you okay my dear, you look a little pale and swilled out.
So are you ready now, to eat this heart and watch the angels shout?
It might seem strange at first but you will soon understand.
So for now just enjoy, the taste of this heart that is damned.

Are you thirsty my dear, I'll pour out some more of me to make you a nice drink.
So I slit open my wrist but there is no blood left to pour.
So I weep you some tears, memories I once lost before.
Now it is done and you begin to see.
You've eaten all of my heart, so what now is the point of me…?

24

Drink the Worry Down

Let's take a further step, now the ground begins to break.
Let's say our actions helped, although we know they were mistakes.
Please try not to worry much, just ease your troubled mind.
Try to look real close, as all your thoughts begin to unwind.

Into a puddle, face first you see the end of the line.
Into the darkness we venture, for another sick and twisted rhyme.
At last you see what it means, but no one's left to care.
You've found the true meaning of life, but now you're out of air.

Just drink the worry down and satisfy all you crave and need.
Let it warm your body, as your soul begins to freeze.
Drink the worry down, and watch the world turn gray.
Just let it go - and watch all your dreams drift away...

Fueling My Addictions

Yes – I like the way it tastes, so sweet on my lips.
I enjoy the awesome high I get, as I give the angel a kiss.
It makes so much sense at the time, yet later it's all just shit.
So I try my very hardest, but I just can't seem to forget.

So forgive me my loves, I did this all for you.
To fuel my passions, and feed my every dream.
So - say what you want to say, think what you want to think.
But I am now what I was always meant to be, *"the demon with angel wings."*

Come on my child, give me your hand and show us some - despair.
Fuel my addictions with more of your pointless screams.
I hold you now and forever, in your every thought and dream.
I've tried my hardest, yet the blame still rests with me...

<u>Absurd</u>

There it goes crashing, the voices into my brain.
The floor starts melting, reality no longer sane.
The dizzy-spell waking, that jittery sound that you make.
I know this is only a beginning but I can't just sit here and wait!

Against the grave falling, all emotions never to replace
Can you taste it, the dust, ash, dirt and memories yet to fade.
It is no mistake, we are at the dawn of a new paradigm.
The ripple continues, within those soft-blue eyes.

I don't want to think it but I can already feel the burn.
Still hoping that someday - I just might learn.
But we can't ignore it, as the worms begin to eat our flesh.
It seems so damn funny - can't help but to laugh…!

There it goes screaming, the child that never was.
Mother tries to help this demon, but you cannot save me now.
The river has over-flown, and now a great lake of fire begins to churn.
So I just laugh within myself, because this place is truly absurd.

<u>I Spat It Out!</u>

I spat it out, the rotten chunks of human meat.
Without a doubt, your heart after all was *truly* diseased.
You were never easy to please, and neither was I.
Now you are dead my love, and I don't even care why…

It just gets to me after a while, the constant bitching and moaning.
I just need to escape, this hell and find some shade.
It's getting to me now, I'm ready for another taste.
It's almost over now, we're just one step away.

I need to shout, to release a little of this strain.
I need to pull it out, this Goddamn rusted blade…
Oh forgive me now, was that not truly what I *meant to say*?
I spat it out, that one last kiss she gave.

Creatures Beneath

The feeling beneath, the ripping-tearing claws that grab hold of me.
The choice that she made, what now left have I to say…?
The question of why, it got so - *fucking old* - after awhile.
So here we go, beneath the dirt for another mile.

The falling beneath, endless I plunge as if there was justice to these fights.
That one choice we made, before we turned off the lights.
To see the better outcome, the dream that sadly has died.
I can now feel it stirring beneath, and I see the Devil in your eyes…

For no justice now, yet onward I spiral as if for a million years.
There's nothing left for us now, God has shed his last tears.
So we dwell in fear, trying to escape that crowded street.
Now I feel them stirring - all the creatures beneath…

A Choice We Made

What better to say, as the pendulum nears with every breath?
It's all been taken away, no time left for a second guess.
Logic is dead, as is all emotion I held for that forgotten love.
I can't believe we've come this far, I can't believe it's already done.

It was a choice we made, to take that foolish step over the edge.
Now the dire consequences, truly are all we have left.
It was a pointless act, to think our love would thrive.
But I just have to laugh, because neither of us survived.

So what would be better to say, only hello – goodbye.
It's all been taken away, but still we had the nerve to try.
Nothing has worked, so now as corpses we know that we have failed.
It was a choice we had made, "to love each other - *if only in hell…*"

Foster Me Hope

Perhaps I'm just sleeping, cold and broken alone on the floor.
It might make sense, if only you would open your eyes.
The door is shut now, "you should've followed the path that was led."
We're all alone now, all alone in our own heads…

Say that you love me, – I KNOW THAT'S A FUCKING LIE!
Please somebody hold me, – THEN LAUGH AS YOU RIP OUT MY EYES!
God gift and give me light, – SO MAYBE I COULD ESCAPE!
Please say there's a chance for hope, – BUT IT IS ME YOU HATE!

Miles below our feet, and only inches beyond the door.
This might just be a dream, as I lie cold and broken raped on the floor.
Shattered and I'm weeping, I am just a worthless whore.
I know I tried my hardest, to maybe be something more.

Now try to say you love me, – I KNOW THAT'S A FUCKING LIE!
Please let me once more hold you, – I CAN'T SEEM TO OPEN MY EYES!
Just gone now and buried, – LOSING ALL WE'VE EVER KNOWN!
I know that it's all a lie, – *but please just foster me some hope*!

Hold Me Closer Satan

Hold me now, I think I'm ready to let these bones decay.
Lonely now, as I see the world has become a darker gray.
It's colder now, no warmth left in this tired soul.
So hold me close, before I melt away with the blood-red snow.

It feels so strange, now you ask me why I was there.
The pain never fades, but no one ever really cared.
It's lonely here, lost forever so dark and broken.
Please hold me close, before the sun fades away.

Not ready now, I just wanted to say I love you one last time.
I tried to tell you how I felt, but I guess I crossed the line.
Now so cold, alone in this world so forever broken.
Please just tell me it'll get better, "please *God* - hold me closer *Satan*…"

Let's Burn the Picture Frame

Let's burn the picture frame and see if the forgotten photo remains.
We've got time to waste, so let's see if we can stand in the flames.
I see the look in your eyes, it truly is sad when a young love dies.
So if you don't like the idea, then please just close your eyes.

Let's burn it all and bathe ourselves in the ashes and grime.
You try to look away, but you're too late this time.
So why try to fight it, just warm yourself with the flames.
I truly am sorry, so sorry that I burned you away.

So let's burn the picture frame to see if we can truly forget.
Let's eat all the ashes, to see if it'll make us sick.
So lost and you can't say that you don't like the fact.
The photo is burning now, no time to turn back.

Let's say that it's all okay and try to make this work.
The flames are growing now, so say goodbye to this forgotten corpse.
We've tried our hardest, but in the end it was all just a waste of time.
So let's burn the picture frame, and laugh as each other dies…

Humans = Insanity

Upsetting the natural flow, now something stirs behind the page.
Small whispers, persistent thoughts dancing their way into the grave.
Now the hours turn, faces caked with dirt and ash.
No more smiles, only pain of the fact that we've all been had.

Give now no more honor, only cold chills and spiteful rhymes.
Taken so low, now this heart not even our God could find.
So make up for it now, but you only want your way.
Forgiveness now forsaken, our souls already in our graves.

Led so far, deep into the middle of a desert of salt.
Try to blame someone else, but you know it is our fault.
Misplaced for so many ages, only to never be found.
I reached out for help, yet you still let me drown…

You Wept For Me.

You wept for me when I didn't come home that night.
You waited for years, and still you sit up at night.
Cold with only the ghosts of the past left to remain.
You lie awake with a torn photo, but it's just not the same.

You tried to say you were sorry and things could change.
Now it's dark out, so dark you just can't find your way.
So try to scream, let the pain go and find release.
You can't run from it any longer, time to set it free.

You wept for me, when I was alone and not to be fixed.
You took me home, and gently cleaned off my filthy wrist.
It was dark out that day, I just could not see.
But I lost it all, "*Cold - Raining*" and the truth is, you have never wept for me…

Irritation of the Mind

Hundreds of demons ripping at my brain from deep inside.
No matter what you say, I've seen it with my own two eyes.
As my eyes had rolled back I began to hear a voice from within.
There's nothing I can do now, I've made the same mistake again.

It's getting old, I just want it the fuck out!
Every time I hold you, this heart fills with doubt.
I can't stand this, the endless pain within my head.
I want it out now, GET IT THE FUCK OUT OF MY HEAD!

Those words, echoes painted to the back of my mind.
Every time I taste that sour burn down my spine.
It gets me every time, the damned feel of going insane.
So I fill my glass with laugher, then drink it down to stop the pain.

Scraping Out My Brain

Dark is this room, the room that's stuck between.
Freezing cold yet so damn hot – can barely breathe.
No words here, mouths sewn shut – can no longer speak.
No words to describe this feeling, so Goddamn bleak.

It feels so bizarre when you tell me that I'm home.
I can't make it out of here – can't lift this old gray stone.
So please tell me, why does this place seem so dark?
It's taking its toll on my soul, tearing it apart.

Pain – that's all we know here, the room stuck between.
Freezing cold, as the crows slowly eat away at me.
No thoughts left, no mind to carry my dreams any more.
It's so dark here because I've scraped out my brain.
Now cold and rotten on the floor……

Chapter 2

Faithless Prayers

Right Place - Wrong Time

I walked in, not ready to see what I saw.
It was a shock to me, to see you've stepped that far passed the line.
The worst part is, I was at the right place, "just the wrong time."

Ages, the way we measure time as it continues to pass us by.
The years gone and wasted but at least I can say I tried.
For there is nothing more I could say, I just wish it would go away.
The image that's forever etched into my mind.

An endless road of rose petals, leading far into the unknown.
And maybe on the other side, there might be a chance for hope.
But then I feel the choke, as my thoughts begin to scream.
Because I was at the right place – only the wrong time.
And you just stared up, surprised to see me.

Hammer the Needle

So hammer the needle deep inside, to numb this fucked up heart.
Laughs shatter against the bare walls, maggots feasting beneath my scars.
The whisper of a bullet, the one at rests in the middle of my brain.
Someday I'll tear it all out, someday you'll understand faith.

Flesh crawling, as I watch the insects pulsing beneath.
On the tip of your beautiful lips, the odd taste of insanity.
It gets to me, the fact that I never got to say goodbye.
We are all gone now, still waiting for it to be our time.

Stuck in an rhyme, but it never makes any sense.
I see now, never ever yet truly it did.
The sick game, sad that it's our lives you threw away.
Forgive me mother and father, "your son has erased his own face."

For nothing now, as my reflection shows only dark.
Hammer the needle to the bone, "*trust me - it's not too far...*"
So give it to me now, fuck up my reality today.
Hammer the needle inside, to numb down all the pain...

Sewing My Wrists

Shaking – breaking – tearing, the small child beaten and bruised.
Lost for what seems like forever, yet still locked in my own room.
Can't get out now, *"FUCK!"* - I AM THE DEVIL YOU HATE!
God forgive me, "I need only a taste," from the fountain of faith.

Can't replace, that awesome sound you made when it felt *just-right.*
Scream now my dear, hard – loud – *soft* – pushing long into the night.
The graveyard sand, flowing rough beneath my tattered flesh.
The *aroma* of her laughter, seeping deep and stealing my breath.

Please help me face it, the fact that I am just a hopeless waste.
I love you my sweet, but now I watch you slip away.
GET ME THE FUCK OUT! Oh is it funny to you my dear!.?
Go on then – push me! See what happens when I snap.

I CAN'T STAND THIS ANY MORE! My love- forgive me.
So please help me as I sew back together my wrist…

Secrets of the Flesh

Listen close to the forgotten ghost, his name is " I ".
Forget me now, " oh if you only knew how," not ready – not ready.
Quiet please, silence now an infectious disease.
Hidden far beyond the secrets of the flesh.

No time – no time, the last credits are beginning to roll.
So hollow within, funny – that I truly had no soul.
I'll take you there, far away where all pains are gone.
Just smile my love – close your eyes and just sing along.

Music is dead, or it could be our hearts are lost.
Too late for a happy ending, no time so just play along.
Just listen close to the forgotten ghost, leading the path into faith.
Can't tell you now - can't tell you now, *"of the secrets hidden behind the page."*

The Zombie Rises

Ages come and gone, *still respect and pride remain within the house of the dead*.
Cool - damp, the morning fog, and the frost covering the text on the stone.
So try to feel it, the awesome touch of the damned.
Laugh now my child, dance in the graveyard till the sun rises once again.

From far beneath, the waking dreamer which never found sleep.
So that is my name, etched there forever on this grave.
Now the ground shakes, it crumbles aside - damp lumps of dirt and grass.
Once more I lift my head, a smile on my face and a rose in my hand.

I am the zombie – try to speak my name if you dare.
Weep not my child, for I am here to ensure your revenge.
Laugh now with pride, remember to keep your head held high.
Take the hand of this zombie, join me into the night.

Scream now all who hold hatred in their hearts.
Fight all you want, soon it shall tear you apart.
There is nothing you can do now, only repent to your lord.
Can he hear you now, from behind that broken door?

This zombie wishes only, to see that smile on the faces of the pure.
My only hope has been, for you to grow strong and valiant in life.
It is time now my friends, let us venture now beyond our faded worlds.
Smile now my children and never fear, *for this zombie rises once again...*

Magic Dust

Upon a golden beach, I lay my head down in hopes of a dream.
It never comes – so how much further until we reach.
Her hand made of thorns, she grips my heart from within my chest.
The acid rains down, corroding all memories, so I just laugh.
Apathy helps, but I still wish she were alive.
It's been decades now, "it might be time to open my eyes."
I see it now drifting by, beautiful clouds made of purple-smoke and ash.
Please hold me real close, until all the emotions of pain have passed.
I love it now, the fact that we are all dead.
So I pull the trigger - and watch the magic dust pour from our heads.

The Jacket

You've got to trust me, I am reaching my hand out for you to take.
No one's there, so all my life I was just a moment too late.
It's at the bottom now, the porcelain face that I adore.
I'm all alone now, lying-naked-broken on the floor.

The walls are softer, yet blood still pours from my mouth.
I cannot speak, for the tiny demons have stolen my tongue.
It makes no sense "I know," still - you've got to save me now.
But I've gotta remember the fact, I'm all alone in this shell.

So on I scream, into the endless void falls all that I've held.
I feel the vomit rising, jagged-rusted bloody-nails.
The walls are frozen, within this place that's lost in time.
But this jacket will keep me warm, while I'm locked here *forever inside...*

Powder Keg

Just about ready, claustrophobic within this tattered shell.
Nothing stops the twitching, so hammer now the remaining nail.
My eyes locked-shut forever and on until the dawn of what's yet to be.
Anger building, constant shouting, "no reasons – only screams."

It's just about ready, now headfirst into the whipping flames.
Take my hand my love, but we are no longer the same.
It's tearing at the back, from deep inside my troubled mind.
I've had enough of this torment, time to erase the line.

Hold me close my love, NOW GET THE FUCK AWAY!
Please tell me we will be alright, then fill this hollow grave.
I love you still and always will, but now I feel it slip.
Don't push me anymore my love, I've had enough of this SHIT!

It's just about ready now, we're at the end looking back.
I can't stand the fact of what you are, just a worthless piece of trash.
So go on then - push me, let's see if you have the gall.
I'm about to snap, and Oh yes – I will kill you all...

The Violins Play On

Upon the soft leaves you lie your head down in awe.
Inevitability seems so grim, no words left to speak at all.
Like a drape it's pulled down-over, then you wonder what it was for.
As you lay your head upon the soft leaves, *waiting to dream forevermore.*

Can't help but sense it, cold chills so numb inside.
Memories of the years you fought so hard – valiant with pride.
Just can't help but say it, that all roads must come to an end.
Memories which linger on, echoes soft upon the wind.

The particulars of the situation so awful, you try not to think.
Inevitability looks you in the eyes, so cold - can barely breathe.
Then you begin to understand, that in the end *"you must make peace."*
As now you begin to realize that your part in this story is done.
So you lay your head back upon the leaves, as the violins play on.

Bullets Within – My Body

Holding closed the jagged wounds on my weary eyes.
Impeding the sad fact that it's all going to spill out.
It begins to flow down and seeps through the cracks on the floor.
Nothing can stop it now, so please hinder this no more…

It's coming to - now all seems such a darker shade of blue.
No words left to speak, so I try my best to explain it to you.
As lying here all day, beneath the starless sky.
I try my hardest to scream but I won't be heard this time.

Scratching furiously my fingernails dig out a bullet from the past.
Thousands and thousands lying just beneath the surface.
Millions and more stuck within my head.
No – can't escape it, the time has come and I am glad you are here.
To watch me fall below, weeping bullets as tears.

Too far to reach back, so many loves burned and erased away.
Can't stop the shaking, rusted bullets in my brain.
Now all is forgotten, yet still I know.
As I pull these bullets from beneath my skin.
Then swallow them down into my soul…

Their Perfect Breed

Am I not a man, trying his hardest to make it through this storm?
Am I not the man, dammed to live in eternal horror?
Was I not a man, when I saved you from falling away?
I guess I truly am, the bastard which you hate…

Am I not a saint, only a martyr whose sacrifices have been forsaken?
Am I not a hero, but only a victim of my own warfare?
Was I not alone that dark night, and did God ever care?
I've done my best, but I am the one you hate…

Am I not a man, leading his children through the dark?
Am I not the man, just a freak left forever lost?
Was I not the man, the great savior that you prayed for to set you free?
I never did fit in this picture, *"for I was never a part of their perfect breed."*

Getting Off My Ass.

Gotta go – gotta go, no time to waste - time to waste.
Waves crashing against a wall, a partition within my brain.
Not to shake it - got no time but we'll make it.
Far beyond – it's been so long, yet I know you don't care.

Freefalling into the pointless push to the other side.
Head first against the brick, then someone turned off the lights.
Now just screaming and shouting, PLEASE GET ME OUT!!!
Now drinking down the poison, and watching the razors bleed out.

Now gotta go – still gotta go, have now no time to waste.
It's killing me – God's killing me, but it's all okay.
No mistake – no mistake, just watch me break – watch us break.
Downfallen dreams now burnt and torn away.

So I've gotta go – gotta go, no time to kill – time to kill…
Nonstop onslaught of the demons hidden within the pills.
So never to heal – nor never to feel, I just need to get off my ass!
Slammed against the wall – the endless voices screaming inside my head.

Broken Mirror

Hidden within a broken mirror, waiting forever for someone to care.
The time has come now, it has indeed been set in stone.
Still I push you away, don't know why I bother to try and be known.
Can't escape this, the blood dripping down onto the dirt.
So I dig myself a little deeper, beneath our dying earth.

So seven years more to go, as I lie here bleeding all alone.
So please mother wake me, "damn the fact that we are all dead."
My love - just try to save me, but no one's left in my head.
Not forgiven for what I've done, so I laugh because the Devil won.
Oh so much fun, as I take hold of the broken mirror in my hand.
I eat it down – digest it all, then vomit up the graveyard sand.

Hidden within a broken mirror, the truth of who we are.
Covered all over this body, millions of meaningless scars.
So we can't deny it, nor try to hide it - seven more years to go…
So exhausted I need to rest this sad and troubled heart.
As I lie hidden within a broken mirror, just beneath these tattered scars.

Drilling Teeth

The drill-bit presses hard, now it begins to twist.
Pushing in deeper, nerves torn, stretched and you can't move a bit.
Screaming now, gargling blood in your throat.
So spit it out, because I don't want you to choke.

The drill pushing deeper, and you feel a pain you've never known.
It hurts at first, then true numbness can be found.
Try just to breathe, you don't want to drown!
The blood is gushing, so go on and spit it out.

Weep me a better melody, and I might make this quick.
Hold on your best, you're starting to look sick.
There is no stopping it, the drill-bit through all of your teeth.
In your throat – gargling blood, "so just spit it out and try to scream…"

The Sleeping Child

A bit cool out this morning, as I walk upon this road once again.
Slightly raining now, freezing razors into these wrists.
The clouds above, a dark gray because they are all dead.
Then the acid falls, drowning this heart with sin.

Running faster, trying to make it to the other side.
The ground breaks open, now falling out of sight.
Out of mind, out of touch with all that ever was.
Forgotten today, as I lie sleeping within your blood.

It's a bit cool out this morning, this cigarette lit – so here we go.
Ten-million more miles, and not one step closer to the truth.
Been trying so hard, I must have forgotten about you.
Forgive me please, I just don't know what else to say.
There's really nothing left, because the sleeping child is now awake.

Grandfather's Pipe

The contour just seems right and makes me feel like I'm whole.
As the smoke is pulled down, deep to my very soul.
Over these long years, so much has changed with time.
But it still makes me calm, as I close both my eyes.

Grandfather was a great man, as I hope to be someday.
Over years this story has evolved but the thought remains the same.
And for that motive, we dance now one step closer to our graves.
Through the haze and growing laughter – until all the pains fade away.

It just makes me feel like a whole man and eases my troubled mind.
The crisp aroma and burning embers inside the old pipe.
So with a smile, each breath fills my heart with pride.
Now that I can see - through grandfather's eyes.

Words Of the Wise

Lick my brain and kiss my eyes, so now you can see.
Taste the bitter rotten poison, known only as me.
So sorry to say, that you too my love – now so fucking diseased.

On no better point so then it just stabs, *"the endless nonsense and constant gab."*
For miles it falls, rusted nails raining into my spine.
Please now tear me open, feast upon whatever's left inside.

The jury can't convict me, "no motive – only rage."
Still you try to judge me, for each sin which I have made.
Just try now to stop this, place your hatred unto me.
Only-now one more step, then this dreamer might find some sleep.

Old Habits

Spoken like a true whore, so tell me now, *"what was it for?"*
All of your games just don't seem to be any fun today.
Why now are you weeping, has someone stolen your face?
So now never to replace, a one single damned word of love...

Listen close to the counterfeit cries of lost ghosts upon the wind.
Their sadness brings a chill to your heart, crawling beneath your skin.
Just can't give it up this time, it's too late to stop this heretic now.
Shaky paintings fall and break, so we are never to be whole again...

Old habits die hard, just can't seem to shake this tradition of sin.
Constant it breaks me, just can't seem to escape what I truly am.
Old loves die hard, and I am sorry our story has come to an end.
I just can't seem to break this habit, of loving the love of sin...

Revolting Revelations

Ranting-raving-ridiculous-revolting-revelations.
Round-ripping-rough-repulsive-regurgitations.
Retarded-resentments-recently-randomly-railed.
Head buried beneath the pavement, eyes burning in the flames of hell.

Laughing-luscious-loony-little-lasting-liberations.
Badly-bent-bones-blossoming-battered-benefactions.
Raped-ripped-rolled-remembering-ravenous-revolutions.
Said-so-sorry-still-steaming-seeming-seriously-scared.

No notifications nudging beyond the pit.
Eyes slit open, bleeding out boiling piles of shit.
Dark-dead-dreams-drowning-down-disappointing-dissatisfactions.
Ranting-raving-relentless-reasons-regarding-ridiculous-revolting-revelations.

Gravel Beneath the Skin

Dragged so far, miles scraping against my tired feet.
Worn down to the bone, so damn scared - can never again bleed.
It's fucking pointless, everything that she just said.
And again it doesn't matter, because we are all already dead.

Pulled down so far, the miles rubbing the flesh raw to the core.
Down goes the whiskey, "*spinning and laughing,*" then head against the door.
For what unseen crimes yet for us to commit.
Grated against the road, gravel beneath the skin.

Hauled so far, kicking and screaming - against my will.
Then I say I'm sorry, yet these wounds can never again heal.
So not to feel bad, only a shit-storm within my brain.
Dragged so far into love, now pulling out the gravel.
Left here alone - in hatred and in pain...

The Wizard's Spell

The answers seem closer, I know that I can almost reach.
The sky becomes darker, something like I've never seen.
All the stars fall from above, raining down broken glass and sand.
Now just so damn out of touch, as if I lost both my hands.

The wizard's spell, locking me in an eternal first-person point of view.
I try to reach out, but then the world melts away - and so do you.
No not a thing can change it, so let's just say that we tried.
She kissed my lips while I was sleeping, I opened my eyes - *then she died.*

Purple lights flickering, faces pressing through the walls.
Fucked up pointless chatter, rampaging down the halls.
Into the far, nowhere that we have not yet already been.
The wizard's spell – *it has me now* – so time to see my face once again.

The answers seem so close, I can almost taste it on my tongue.
The sky has become a memory, now faded out and done.
The potion tastes so twisted, then a smash and now we see.
She said on that day that she loved me but then we both awoke from our dreams.

Skull Fucked

I hate this world and everybody in it.
I hate this life, I wish I could just end it!
I hate this place, in which I'm somehow stuck inside.
I hate your face and all your fucked up lies!

I hate all the nonsense that seeps from your twisted brain.
I hate your kisses, every time they cause me pain.
I hate the way, you say that you care for me so much.
I truly hate the fact, that I am now and forever - skull fucked!

I hate the movement of the little demons beneath the flesh.
I hate the taste, of your nasty decaying rotten breath.
I hate that you tell me, that I mean to you so much more.
I hate that I'm so skull fucked, still pining over that worthless whore…

Tasting the Black Flames

Take me there - and leave me forever and always lost.
Leave me frozen, blanketed in layers of shit and frost.
Say that you love it, then ride me hard into the night.
Step out onto the ledge – let it all go and then say goodbye...

Just run a little faster, through the field of mushroom screams.
Down now above the cloud – where God and the Devil dream.
We taste the black flames, and our souls become alive.
We look each other in the eyes, and then laugh as we both die.

Take me there – a million miles passed our great blue sky.
Far out beneath the water, waves pushing side to side.
You taste the black flames, that burn within my soul.
I feed to you all my troubles, now they keep you so cold.

Just about over, locked in the closet holding a blade.
Echoes of weeping-laughter, clouding my fucked up retarded-brain.
So please take me there and just leave me for dead.
Again we taste the black flames that are burning out in both our heads...

Knuckle Shift

Be careful what you say, knuckles shift and crack against the bones.
What are you trying to say, with my hands so tight around your throat?
Nothing left to do now but bury you beneath six feet of mud.
Come on then – just push me, and let's watch it all come undone...

Be happy that you're breathing, come on - just count to ten.
Step off or get ready, another corpse beneath the sand.
I never meant to offend you, no – no *"Oh yes I did..."*
Fuck it all - just get ready, now knuckles begin to shift.

Push back a little harder, maybe next time you might draw some blood.
Within your little brain, stupidity becomes a raging flood.
So let's get it straight, for this one last damned time.
But be careful what you say, knuckle shift and you're out of time...

Remembering to Forget

Last words unspoken, then the world begins to slip.
Into a darker shadow, inside the open stitch.
And oh that kiss, still haunting this exhausted mind.
So now another step taken, far - far passed and beyond the line.

It is colder now here, no sign of hope in sight.
It might not be so dark, if someone would just turn on the lights.
Then it comes rushing back faster, causing so much pain.
As I see you again when I close my eyes, *"still those smiles drive me insane."*

Last words unspoken, because we just didn't take the time.
So now you might understand why, as your spine begins to itch.
Lost loves lingering on, in a sung song in which I dearly miss.
So as I look you in the eyes my love, I remember to forget…

"And then our world just fades away."

A Twisting Blade

A twisting blade dug deep into my side.
These eyes turn gray, and then reality slowly dies.
I try to keep a grasp on the world, yet I'm already stuck in space.
The blade twists in deeper, so I laugh it all the same.

As I've tried once to tell you, I am the bastard you hate.
My dear I truly loved you and still you cast me away.
Then you fed me to the wolves and smiled as I screamed.
You've taken my heart, now no blood left for me to bleed.

A twisting blade dug far into my aching side.
I don't want to see this, so just rip out both my eyes!
You say that I'm too weak, and yes that might be true.
Again you twist the blade in deep, bringing me closer to my tomb.

Dig Deeper

Dig deeper into my eye-socket to get at my brain.
Pull it out one piece at a time, and yes it tastes insane.
Dig deeper into these filthy wrist, now open so wide.
The maggots pulse as they pour out, then become demonic butterflies.

Breaking apart each day now, can't hold it together anymore.
Then the vomit comes up, and down onto the floor.
It's steaming, chunks of rotten bloody human meat.
Then I have to laugh, because I've been eating only me.

Dig deep into the darkest section of my past to find.
I truly was happy, once upon a time.
Now just a reject, a worthless waste of cries and pains.
Just dig yourself deeper, to get out of my brain…

I Thought You Cared…

I thought that you would be there for me - guess I was wrong.
An eternity passed - I turned to ash, but I guess it was all my fault.
Now I try to open my broken eyes to see what I've done to hurt you.
I thought that you would be there, but now I'm alone in my own tomb.

You once told me that I was a great man, yet now that is all passed.
You once said that you loved me, but now in my face you just laugh.
I once thought that I could save her, from this sad world of pain.
But I guess I only hurt her more, so now in this purgatory I wait.

I thought that you would be here, standing at my side with pride.
I truly am alone here, no sights to embrace with my shattered eyes.
Only shame holds the answer, but I just wanted her to smile.
I thought that she would love me, even passed the end of time.

I hope that you might hear this, all my screams of pain.
I wish that I could have saved you, but now yesterday has been erased.
I thought that you would be there for me, to save me from all my fears.
Now I weep blood as I sit here alone – *"and I thought that you cared…"*

They Choke Our Dreams

They choke our dreams and say that it's all for the best.
This world grows dark with no heart left to beat inside my chest.
It falls even darker, the fact that we are beaten down.
I hate them so much, yet I love them all – OH GOD GET ME OUT!

They say that they need us to just understand respect.
Yet they judge us all, spit in our face and then throw us aside.
So please now tell me why, has all of this pain been caused by me?
They say that they love us, and then choke our one lasting dream.

Just leave let us be, because we want only to see beyond the page.
Please hold us with care, and then we're thrown down in fear.
But somehow I know this pain has all been caused by me.
I love you all and hate this world, because they've killed our dreams…
"Yet all that we have ever wanted, was only to be free."

El Cu Cuy

The emotion's revolving, the hatred's evolving.
I know now that I've become something I never wanted to be.
The laughter is seeping, this bastard is sinking.
Deeper into my own fears and I know now only pain.

Her smile did sooth me, all her kisses consumed me.
Now I only wish that we were not both in our graves.
The time is constant wasting, in my heart I'm constantly pacing.
And as we touch - her smile decays, becoming only ash and dust.

She was such an *Angel*, I tried to find a better angle.
Yet in the end I still fell deep into this nightmare called life.
There is something stirring and now I feel it burning beneath my flesh.
Truly I am the monster you wish to destroy.

Please now say you love me and take me far from this emotion called pain.
I tried my hardest my love to protect you.
Yet in the end I could just never keep you safe.
So now the laughter seeps inside *and yes*, "I am the monster you hate…"

Chapter 3

Looking Through the Hole.

Revolt of the Anarchist

I don't want to and I never did, put up with this world of shit.
I can't stand to and never will, understand their pointless lies.
Just anarchy now, as I pray unto the world an endless pain.
Until it drives you insane, _then you might be able to see through my eyes._
So I stand now with hatred, and speak from my heart with pride…

Push not the children of the world, for we shall rise and take control.
Stand up now my brothers and sisters and let us escape this bitter cold.
Just chaos and disorder - leading our path today.
I don't want this fight or this life, but I must make a stand.
True justice will be found, when this anarchist rises once again.

Disgrace and shaky laughs between each word that we speak.
A path that we've been following for what seems like an eternity.
Now I push so hard, just to get you out of my face.
So I watch you fall deeper now into your hole and maybe I was right.
I can't stand this fucked up reality but I shall stand up now and fight…

The Agony of Defeat

Alone now broken in shame, lying in the middle of the road.
Just waiting for a ride, far away from this city of _"Untruth & Pain."_
And every day I have to live with the fact, that I am only a waste.
I just don't want to accept it, the fact of my defeat.

All alone here, lying in the middle of a crowded room.
Smoke rolling off my tongue, then the whiskey begins to consume.
With a clove burning behind my itchy eyes, I begin to see.
Even though I'm all alone, still the Devil has a hold on me…

So I just can't let it be, I can't believe that I tried so hard only to lose.
It's all gone now, dust and memories in our forgotten past.
Oh and how I wished those emotions would never pass.
But now it's done and there is truly nothing more for me to say.
I just need to come to terms and accept it, the agony of defeat.

On Your Knees

On your knees whore, open your mouth and close your eyes.
On second thought, look up at me and don't you dare blink...
There are some things that get to me after a while.
So for now I need you to just shut the fuck up!

On your knees bitch, you know that this is truly what you want.
Oh I am so sorry, I never meant to show the world who you are.
So now they see, what a precious little waste of laughter and smiles.
I want to say I care, but I won't fucking lie!

On your knees slut, I just can't believe what you have become.
But I guess it's all my fault, and I am the only one to blame for all of this.
I just want the constant noise and bullshit to stop.
So get on your knees, so I can shut you the fuck up...!

Please Oh Please: Kill Me...

See me alone – with only hate, now I know the voices are alive.
Please tell me now before it's too late, "and damn we're out of time."
So reach in far, the wooden box holding a great forgotten truth.
Please hold me close before this is over, "and damn I lost you too."

So need I see - need I die, would you care - would you cry?
The violins play on, the piano begins to add shape to the melody.
And it's hidden so far inside of me, the blade next to my spine.
Please just tell me - that one thing, the reason behind the rhyme.

Oh not to worry yourself, the sun will rise once again.
Then we awake to darkness and live out our lives in dread.
I can't stand the fact that I'm *lying here forgotten* in someone else's head.
It's just so damn funny, "and we won't get a second chance."

Now all I need is to see, beyond that ledge – a mile down.
Now all I want is to leave this place, and let my demons out.
So need I see - need I die, would you care - would you cry?
Just please Oh please, somebody kill me...

54

Shit & Hammers

Can't let myself forget, then again it all starts to slip.
I think I'm gonna be sick, someone please save me from this rage.
It burns beneath the skin - all our pointless sins.
Can't help but to know that all the blame rests with me.

Millions of voices rapidly screaming all throughout my brain.
So I dig deep within myself in front of a mirror.
I just wish I could remember my face, *"Just wish I could forget her name?"*
And on goes the shit storm, hammering on my grave.

I won't let us fade, and yet we are gone now for eternity.
I can't stop the screams, they make me feel just so alive.
I can't stop the tearing, peeling my flesh off with a knife.
I love this Goddamn torment, stuck forever in my mind.

Can't let myself forget now, I've come too far down this road.
I wish I could have saved us, but that morning - it got too cold.
I just need to stop this, all the aches that build up in me.
And again it rains down *Shit & Hammers*, so never again will I sleep…?

Religious Defects

God doesn't speak to us anymore, or maybe we've just all gone deaf.
Still you try to judge me, as you place your knife into my chest.
But all I really want to say, is that I need to get away.
Before you nail me upside down on a burning cross…

Then on your knees you pray, hoping it won't leave a stain.
All your scars prove that you are just as wicked as I…
And it is a fact you just can't deny, so maybe you should walk away.
Into a deeper level of Hell, so that you may purify yourself in the flames.

God is laughing up there, at this sick and distorted game.
And on you drag yourself in, but really only every other Sunday.
And I just find it so damn funny, that you still try judging me.
But I don't think God can hear you down there.
While you're on your knees…

Crimson-Beast

The monster is now – here and it is waiting.
Darkness – it grows, now tomorrow is wasted.
Time it is losing, we can no longer stop the screams.
On and on it goes, echoing far into my pain filled dreams.

Just can't seem to shake it, then I begin to shake all night.
It's too damn hot out, yet here I'm frozen in ice.
You point your fingers and laugh at it, the one who resides in shame.
I guess I can no longer fight it, the fact of what I was meant to be.

Still it gets dark here at night, as if all the stars and moons simply died.
And so we push our way out of the storm, just maybe to be free.
But I just can't fight it anymore, so go right ahead and condemn me.
And as I stand here in the flames of *Hell* I laugh as I realize.
I am the crimson beast…

The Masterpiece

Words – that's all that you seem to be looking for.
A new group of words that just might give us a little hope.
So let's cure this illness with laughter.
Because life after all, was nothing more than a joke.

Passion – it seems so funny that you remain as what you are.
In the back of this poet's head, a fucked up jagged scar.
It gets to me, and then I know that rage remains within.
Can't find the words this time, so be quiet as you step off the ledge.

Colder now - it is just too cold, I can't feel my arms.
I'm burning here, as all the acid bleeds out of my rotten heart.
But I'm better for it, and I know now how it feels to be frittered away.
Oh and you with that bullet-hole in the middle of your forehead.
Now that - was the true masterpiece.

A Real Fuck You!

It was a choice lain out, a choice for both me and you.
Then you couldn't decide, so I guess in the end we had to lose.
And here it stands now, the face that I wish would just die.
I want it gone already, yet I haven't even opened my eyes.

It was a lie we told, each time we kissed each other's lips.
Then I have to remember, that our game of lust was truly sick.
But I only want to stop it, this Goddamn pointless rant.
Once more I have to ask you my love, to just end all the fucking gab!

No not much more for me to say, as I lie here so dazed and beaten.
Leaning my head out of the window, and damn it's starting to rain.
The end of our story, it was a choice – a choice we just had to choose.
So the only statement I have left now, would have to be a real **FUCK YOU**!

Now the Phantoms Fade

Hollow in this mind, now just so alone.
Still a man of pride, as I lie here nailed and so broke.
Trying to gaze up, yet there's nothing more to see.
Down here so hollow, left here so alone and bleak.

Now it begins to push to the side – it's dark now, I scream.
Alone here a mile down, never again now shall I dream.
I just want to save me, but I know that I am damned.
Please get me out of this, take me away once again.

I only want to laugh, and to see that smile on your face.
Soon tomorrow will fail, so all we had was yesterday.
I need only to feel you hold me, close because I am so cold.
Get me out of here, just bury me in a bottomless hole.

Another drink, then it slowly begins to feel okay.
It slips to the side again, the torment of being insane.
So Goddamn alone here, it seems that no one remains.
I am forever alone, as now the phantoms fade.

Nail Me With a Screw

Push me uneven, deeper falling into a salt filled grave.
Now it seems so seamless, all the corruption within my brain.
I like the way it takes me down there, into the loss of grip.
I love it – but can't seem to move, so I laugh out loud as I trip.

The walls are spinning, but the truth is – that it's me.
All my flesh is melting, and my bones seem so bleached.
I shake now with that jittery voice, the voice that never sounds.
Want only to reach out but I can't move, and then deeper I sink down.

She took me there to the other side once, I lost myself for years.
We took a drink from the fountain, it tasted like laughter and fear.
It's all so funny, as we dance around in circles watching passion bloom.
I just can't seem to move from here, guess you nailed me with a screw.

So uneven, I tripped over my own feet and slammed my head.
She tasted the blood from off my face, then she told me to do it again.
The haze it is growing, and I love this blissful sense of insanity.
No longer can I move now, for the screw is nailed so deep within me.

Mushroom Tea

My head is spinning and I just can't see.
These lungs are caving in, no longer can I breathe.
My skin it is burning, as I'm placed beneath the ice.
Can't shake it but I feel as if I'm drowning, so much deeper in me.
"All this as I swallow down the very first sip, of this delicious *Mushroom Tea…*"

My faith is like a clay – so distortedly molded.
My face has been erased, and I don't think anyone will remember.
So I laugh as I pull tiny slivers of gold from out of my eyes.
Now that she's gone, I don't even know why it still gets to me.
"Then dizzy I lean back and take my second sip, of this delicious *Mushroom Tea...*"

Her eyes they become bitter, as we swim in this river of laughter.
My body begins to tremble, and I'm just waiting for it to pass me.
I do love it when you push me harder, then you softly bite my neck – *"I scream!"*
World spinning-melting round and round in circles as she dances for me.
And I have to smile as here we drown, in an ocean of *Mushroom Tea…*"

Standing Under a Ladder

Bullshit I say, it was all because of the drink that tasted so sweet.
Just torment I say, as I so enjoy the pleasure of both you and me.
But it is darker now, here as I rest myself on the ground.
Realizing I'm standing beneath a ladder, knowing it could all come crashing down.

Any moment I say and as we walk away, I know there must have been a point.
Anytime today, and as we go insane, I so love the blissful burn of your touch.
Then I have to admit that I am truly fucked, and it's all because of me.
So here I am standing under a ladder, waiting for it to all fall upon me…

Just bullshit I say, and that's all you've ever thought of me.
I was only a lonely bastard, hoping for a better dream.
Now luck is shot, and forever locked deep in the back of my heart.
So as I stand here under a ladder, I watch myself slowly fall apart…

Watching the Atoms Decay

As I lay here and watch all the atoms slowly decay.
I have to smile because it's about fucking time.
Then yesterday begins to fade, so in the end I hope we had a great time.
As I lay here in an open grave, I watch the stars and moon painfully die.
Weeping as all the atoms decay – "everything decays here in my mind…"

As now, just give me a smile and make me feel like I'll be okay.
Please whisper something into my heart before it too begins to decay.
"No – No My love!" There must be a way we can survive this break.
Here as I lie screaming and watching all our atoms decay.
So far away and please my love, just tell me I don't have to open my eyes.

Watching the world begin to end, I say again it's about fucking time!
Loving the way she gently holds me tight and then we both close our eyes.
To maybe save ourselves from breaking down and being forgotten.
But all I want is for you my love to kiss my lips as our world fades away.
I love you so and now it's over, as all our atoms have now decayed.

Sewing My Face Over Yours

You are so precious, I adore you in every possible way.
You taste so sweet, on my tongue when you kiss my lips.
You truly are the one who is holding my heart in your hands today.
It feels so soft and warm, when I gently touch your face.

You speak the simple nothing that I needed to hear tonight.
You are the new motive, in which I've been searching to find.
You truly are the prettiest angel to take my hand and lift me away.
It feels so blissful, when you rest your cheek upon my face.

So now the hours are spilling and darkness is filling my heart with pride.
Then it all goes so much faster, when we turn off the lights.
I just can't speak it, I only want us to scream!
As I place my fingers on your face, laughing at our lustful needs.

You are so precious, I only wish to gaze upon you for ages.
Until Death comes and tells me that it is time to return home.
As never shall I be alone, as I hold this reflection known as you and me.
I sew my face over yours so we can be precious.
"We are so precious now – can't you see...?"

When the Last Dragon Dies

When the last dragon dies, I don't want to say goodbye.
Because that would be admitting that all hope is dead...
When the last word is spoken will anyone be left to hear?
Humanity is truly over, I see it now and know it clear.

When the first kiss is forgotten, I don't want to realize.
Because that would be admitting that last kiss draws near.
When all of this world is forgotten and the universe finds peace.
I hope God will know - that at least we tried...

When the first touch is felt, it leaves a bit of a shock.
When the last touch grows cold, all hope is lost.
Because we know now that all the beautiful *fall leaves* are truly dead.
We are all just *fallen leaves*, blowing in the wind.

Passion & Lust

A fire is hottest when first lit, *passion & lust*, joyful-sins.
On now into a greater hoping as she takes my hand.
It really should get to me but it feels so good to be so bad.
And she bites my lip, in pleasure I begin to bleed.
She spoke so softly, those sounds of passion, lustful-screams.

On now deeper down the hall into the room at the very back.
"Then somehow we both end up on the floor."
Laughter ringing, in the dizzy trip of spinning smoke and purple fire.
Lustful actions as we lay there, in the air a haze of the delicious smoke.
Then her eyes gaze so deep into mine.

Passion & lust, as together the night becomes a day.
She bites my neck and draws blood, just because she loves the taste.
And she places her hand on my chest and listens to my heartbeat.
Passion starting to overrule - as lust does the very same.

Make a Difference

Straight to the bone, just to prove I was right.
A long walk down a short road, in the middle of the night.
I don't know why I always seem to be the one who fails.
I loved them all once, but now I burn in hell.

Did I make a difference or only fuck it up even more?
Would it make a difference if I learned how to entertain that bore?
Will it make a difference if I say that I tried my best?
Does any of this make a difference or is it all just a waste of breath?

So on the candles burn, but I know now I am truly alone.
So I lie down in the middle of the room just waiting for some hope.
And it never comes so I'm just lying here drunk and weeping.
As gallons of laughter spews up and onto the ground.

Did I make a difference when I offered up my heart?
Would it make any difference if I didn't know that you tore it apart?
Will this make any difference or is it all just a waste?
I need to make a difference, and yet again I'm erased...

Wisdom-Tooth

How much longer do I have before I wake up dead?
Just try to listen to the gab that dances on my breath.
So go on and take my hand and let's step over the ledge.
Come on and scream then, because it's all in our heads.

Pushing hard and causing a pain we've never known.
It breaks through the skin, and bleeds out from my very soul.
And I only want this to make sense, beyond all the pain.
I am truly a sin, I was God's greatest mistake…

How much further will it grow from beneath the flesh?
On and on it goes, bringing me closer to death.
Just want to say that it might all be alright.
It's too late now, so just turn off the lights.

It pushes further from beneath the gum.
Blood pouring on the ground as this bastard loads the gun.
I just need it out, it's causing too much ache.
So I rip out this wisdom tooth with my fingers, then throw it all away…

The Insect That Matters

I've been forgotten, so-so many times and more.
I've left this reality, as I lied there screaming on the floor.
I wanted the answers, but never did have a question to ask.
So I lie here on the ground, waiting for this bullshit to pass.

I've seen the darkness, every time I gaze into the mirror.
I've felt the heartache, as now I weep alone here in fear.
I wanted to save us but lost it all yet again.
I was once the insect that mattered, now only a forgotten sin.

I've held the hand of a corpse and she said I was a great person.
I've let this all run its chores, yet found no better purpose.
There was once a time when we all laughed and played.
I want only to be the insect that matters, but I've been stepped on.
So now I am nothing more than a stain…

Suck it Hard

I need you now, get on the ground, come on bitch just suck it hard.
Just look up now into my eyes and give me that smile, *that smile so sweet.*
Suck it hard, just do it good because right now that's all I need.
To get me through this fucked up day, *so come on girl get on your knees.*

I need you now, please hold me close then get the fuck away from me.
I love it – yes – when you say that nothing and it feels just right.
Come on and look up at me then close your fucking eyes.
Because it does not matter, I only need this to get me through the night.

Suck it hard so maybe I can release a little bit of this stress.
Just get naked bitch, because I don't want you to fuck up your dress.
Suck it hard so all the poison can bleed out and I'll for once feel okay.
Just suck it hard – tell me you love me – then get the fuck away…

While She Danced

While she danced I had to laugh, because she was dancing for me.
I sat back and had a drink, the music loud as she danced for me.
Rhythms moving the air so soothing, almost as if it were a dream.
But now I just have to smile, as I sit back and she pours me another drink.

While she danced I was at peace, because it was our song.
While we laughed and enjoyed our drinks, I just had to sing along.
The rhythms pushing, as she moved so gracious with the beat.
And as she kissed me I had to smile, while she danced for me.

Time has stopped now but for only a moment.
So in this moment I have to just try to hold on.
Oh I love the intoxicating way she moves her hips along with the beat.
Then she smiles and takes my hand, so now together it feels so neat.
Indeed I have to say, *"I love it when the music plays, and how she dances just for me…"*

A Frozen Spider

So on goes the distorted torments that never seem to cease.
A frozen spider on the tip of my tongue, making my body feel so weak.
Venom locked within my brain, causing so - very much pain.
So on goes this Goddamn torment making me feel so fucking insane.

Useless now as I always was and I guess I forever will be.
A frozen spider inside my lungs making it so very hard to breathe.
And I just can't see, any way to stop this from becoming our hell.
I want only to hold you close, I took that step and then I failed.

So on goes the constant torment known now as you and me.
A spider hiding within my heart, frozen now and left so bleak.
I've tried my best and still I lost everything I held close to me.
A frozen spider on the tip of my tongue, so I bite it off.
Now never again shall I speak...

Holding the Veins Closed

I'm holding the veins closed, the blade mustn't have been sharp enough today.
Maybe it is for the best, well - at least that's what I would like to say.
And I wish it would all go away, so I can rest my tired head.
I'm holding the veins closed, so I might not wake up dead.

And dead I awake to the same old shit that you spew from your face.
I don't want to think it, but all the love has been thrown away.
So I'm trying to see it through and hoping the sun might rise.
I'm holding the veins closed, too afraid to even open my eyes.

I'm trying my best now, to not become the asshole again.
Maybe on another level, I truly want it all to end up like this.
But still I'm trying to keep these veins closed so I don't just bleed dry.
I'm holding the veins closed, just hoping I'll survive.

Beyond this bitter logic, of dumb asses that don't know shit.
I'm holding the wound closed, the open gash on my wrist.
And maybe I might be missed, but I know that's not true.
Still I'm holding these veins closed, *but I'm only doing it for you...*

64

Every Other

She said I was a great person...
Every other character in this story thinks I'm just a piece of shit.
She wanted me to hold on and smile, *so I held her close and gave her a kiss.*
Every other character in this story told me I was only a waste.
She told me to hold on, because the sun will shine for another day.

I wanted to take that step over and just watch it all fall away.
Every other time I tried to save us, it always ended the same.
I needed only to get away, before I speak or do something I don't mean.
She said I was a great fighter, yet every one else tells me I'm weak.

I hope someday that this all just might make a little sense.
Every other time I tired to help, it always ended in sin.
She wanted me to be happy and to just smile, *"because it is going to be okay."*
Every other time I felt this broken, they all just threw me away.

She said I was a great person and asked me what I was thinking.
I told her that the truth is, *"I wish I knew how to cry..."*
She told me to keep on trying, because I am stronger than the rest.
But every other time I tried to save us, it always ended in death....

KeyHole

Standing at the door, elevated voices screaming on the other side.
It is so painful, as I just stand here biting my lip till it bleeds.
Unable to say a thing, as my greatest friend's heart is put to the test.
And I still don't know why, I just stood there holding my breath.

Now forced to do the one thing I dread the most.
And to sacrifice all, as now I can only cast everyone away.
I'm just standing there at the door and through the keyhole I see.
That the truth is that I am the Devil and the world does hate me.

Through the keyhole I see, the grim fact of the blade across the wrist.
And oh she laughed – oh she laughed, as the blood drained onto floor.
I can't believe that I just stood there, right on the other side of the door.
I said only nothing, because it was never my war to fight.
So I stood there, my lip bleeding as I silently screamed on the other side.
As I looked through the keyhole and watched my best friend's heart die.

Love Poems

Hands stretched out a million miles and still can't reach.
Trying to find the right words, as now growing weak.
Alone here on the floor, blood dripping off the tip of my tongue.
Echoing memories of her face, so with each teardrop I load the gun.

Hollow now and always, as I awoke with that taste in my mouth.
The burn ligers on, as all my inner voices constantly shout.
I need it out, so please save me from this reflection named Me.
Hold me close my love, help me set my heart free.

My hands stretched out, a million years and still yet to know.
I've felt the touch of an angel, and it remains within my soul.
All the jittery movements that keep me awake at night.
Still I ask you to save me, save me from this night.

My arms held open, and there is no one here for me to embrace.
Only these pointless poems I scrape off the top of my brain.
I've asked you real nicely, *"please guide me out of this hell."*
And I'll recite you another love poem, as we both watch my heart fail…

Thumbtack

I've wept all the tears there are to weep.
I've bled all the blood there is to bleed.
I've died all the deaths this soul could endure.
Still I lie here waiting, hoping to learn.

Now and always, just so numb and jaded.
Laughing loco and feeling so pasted.
For times and times I know I've wasted.
The lips of that angel, I know I have tasted.

I've taken all the shit this mind can take.
I've waited too long, I can no longer wait.
I've said all of which there is for me to say.
Still I just want this, to hurry up and fade.

Now we've come too far, so no time to look back.
You tasted my scars and then we both laughed.
You have stolen all of that which was once me, so now I can't react.
So I stay here stuck to your walls, with a fucked up rusted thumbtack.

I See It Now…

I see it now as I begin to drown, I am the forgotten meek.
I feel it now within my heart, our God has truly forsaken me.
But it is alright and you should not worry yourself my dear.
I see it now as I begin to drown, the release of my last breath of air.

I see it now as I fall asleep, all the lights fading away.
I know it now within my soul, I shall truly never be saved.
But it is okay, all of this torment we must endure in this war.
I see it now beyond the clouds, the truth hidden behind that door.

I see it now as I begin to drown, you laughing at my disgrace.
I feel it now - the stab within, as all of this world now turns gray.
And it will never fade, "so I might as well enjoy this pain."
I see it now and hear it loud, as God and the Devil both weep…

I Love You My Child

I love you my child, you need not fear while I'm at your side.
I love you my child, you look so tired so just close your eyes.
Let all your dreams become alive today and forever more.
Relax your mind my child, just set yourself free.
I will love you my child always, and so I'll keep you safe in harmony.

I love you my child, so I'll help you grow strong through the years.
I love you my child, so I'll wipe clean all your aching tears.
Let the sound of *Peace* ring on within your heart till the end.
Smile now my child, today is a great day for joy.
I love you my child, *"so just close your eyes and let your dreams lift you away."*

Beyond so much more than the path of leaves seems to lead.
Deeper into a commitment, and unconditional devotions of the heart.
And time and time again it keeps on growing, as the sands flow so constant.
"It seems as if we have only a moment to embrace this gift of life."
I love you my child very much so – but it is time now to open your eyes.
"Welcome to the world…"

Chapter 4

Finders Keepers.

Respect the Demon

No time left for reason, so just laugh with me – laugh with me.
There is now no more time left, *"this is the end of all things to be."*
So there's nothing left to say, to make it go away.
And still the memories of then never seem to dissipate.

It all truly feels the very same, when tomorrow never seems to arrive.
Then you know beyond any doubt, that our love was truly contrived.
So do you now feel alive, or is this just another day awake in your hell?
There's no time left for second guesses, *"your heart now too overwhelmed."*

Just show some respect, you are in presences of the end to come.
Hold yourself close, so you don't get lost as you come undone.
Please laugh with me – just laugh with me, as our world slowly ends.
You must respect this demon, if ever we're to make amends.

I Know You Are

I know you are - the one that kept me from pulling the trigger.
I know I am - the one that failed at saving our love.
I know in my heart - we cannot stop us from losing ourselves.
I know you are - the one that torments me as I burn in hell.

The truth must be - there is no better way to end this tome.
As above now I swing - watching the rope stretch out and rip.
There is no one now - I must really be sick.
So on now I face the fact - of what our love was damned to be.

I know you are - there with me as I wander through the dark.
I know I am - beaten, bruised and perpetually scared.
I know there is - a way that I can stop this all from ending the same.
I know you are - the voice in my head that keeps telling me, *"I am insane."*

Spoon Full of Ash

Can't stand these pills, as they roll down the back of my throat.
These wounds can never heal, so in my own blood I soak.
Straight to the core of this soul and then deeper within.
I can't stand the taste, as it drips down the back into my head.

Then for miles it takes me, these roads that never seem to end.
And for years we venture on, into the motives of our every sin.
So we can't just deny it, the grim fact that we are insane.
I hate the way it tastes, the bitter pills that bring on the shame.

I can't bear the lonely fact now, I only wanted you to smile.
I've torn this life away, and found no better means.
The director called cut, but we must not be done with this scene.
Oh God I can't stand the taste, as it slowly burns its way inside.

Can't stand these mushrooms, as they tell me to kiss her lips.
I won't put up with this nonsense, "*I've had enough of this shit!*"
Just can't see through the smoke, as our photos burn - permanently erasing our past.
Hoping it just might help a bit, "*I swallow down*" - this bitter spoon full of ash.

Lost & Alone

Here in this room, the room so cold and broken.
Pure solitude here, in my own personal rat infested hellhole.
I lie my body down, and then smash my head against the floor.
You don't understand but that was always the problem we had before.

Here in this room, the space that's lost between.
Between reality and my nightmares, fears that go on unseen.
And so I call out, but no one's there to reply.
I am truly alone here now, lost with nothing but my mind.

Here in this room, the purgatory I've kept for me.
Pure insanity can be acquired, "*just have to let it all free.*"
Then open eyes now and so very cold as I call out into the abyss.
Only shadows remain, *with lingering memories I am damned to forget…*

My Hummingbird

My hummingbird, tell me now – *"why so frantic here today?"*
It's been so long and I have to laugh because it has still yet to change.
So now lifting higher, into the golden clouds and heaven stars.
Just hold on my love and sing our song, my beautiful hummingbird

My hummingbird, why is it so cold there where you are?
Can you hear my voice as I speak, can you feel the depth in all my scars?
It's been sometime -yes- and still I wish only to hold you dear.
As together we sing our song, and feel the peaceful music so clear.

My hummingbird, why is it that you seem so weak.
So pale and exhausted, maybe you need to eat.
It is much harder now, still she tries to break through to the other side.
Just trying to leave, *hoping only to acquire a golden sunrise and some faith.*
So I hold you close and kiss you my love.
Then smile as I watch my hummingbird fly away…

Love Note Ashes

Smoke filling the room, it's getting hard to see.
The smoke still filling the room, getting hard to breathe.
And still I stare into the *blackened flames* watching the past being erased.
Burning and burning, all these love notes addressed to me.

The fire has gone out, still smoke lingers in the air.
So I breathe it all in, then exhale all my past years.
So much time spent, and never there was a thing to gain.
Miles upon miles taken, now only 1,000 miles of pain.

Smoke still lingering, the cigarettes are just about out.
So I'm left now with only ashes, ashes of the once that could never be.
I take a hand full of the *burned love notes* then swallow it down and scream.
So I know I shouldn't have and yet I did, laugh at the death of our dream.
"Now I vomit out the ashes of all the love notes, she had ever addressed to me."

What it Looks Like...

What it looks like, is a lump of rotten flesh and tar.
What if feels like, I am just too numb to describe.
Now we just can't deny it, as rage pours from this mind.
What it looks like is a child, too afraid to open its eyes.

What it seems like, is a chance that has truly failed.
What it looks like, is a Goddamn worthless reject from hell.
So here we go now, one step or more beyond the page.
Still can't realize, we'll never truly escape this cage.

What it feels like, is a coldness this world has never known.
What it sounds like, is a zombie as it first begins to moan.
What it stands for, is a truth we won't ever fully admit.
What it looks like inside my heart, is a fucked up world of shit!

Luna's Kiss

So I lay my head back, and she places her lips on mine.
So I reach out, but she's already holding me tight.
I try to speak my emotions, yet have no voice that sounds.
She holds me close when I need her, she truly loves me without a doubt.

Luna's kiss, it tells my heart that I'm never alone.
Luna's smile, it shines and fills the world with light.
Luna's touch, so blissful as she runs her fingers through my hair.
Luna's kiss, melting away all the pointless despair.

So I lay my head back, here in this open grave.
So I reach out, but there is no hand there for me to take.
So I laugh, knowing I'll truly never be missed.
So as I close my eyes for sleep, I smile as I remember *Luna's kiss...*

Nine Lives

There it falls – so sorry I couldn't save us this time.
Again we break, as we take another step over that line.
Then feet pulled out from beneath us, and headfirst into the dirt.
I am just truly so sorry and still you laugh as I burn.

Nine lives to live - well I guess that might make a little sense.
I really don't know where it is I'm going anymore, and I guess I never really did.
That is my damned luck, and again I plunge headfirst into this war.
I'm so sorry I couldn't save us this time.
Then again I fall – and now eight lives more…

The Voice That Failed

What now, as the broken glass begins to seep through the flesh.
I have only to scream, as I begin to slit both my wrists.
Then I want that… to step over the ledge - a mile down.
I want only to breathe under water, and never to drown.

I was once a hero, there to save the day and win their hearts.
I was once a fighter, but now I'm gone, yet still waiting to depart.
I need to stop this and yet on I go, never to end in this tormented hell.
I weep laughter as I rip off my face, *"Just don't know why it is I do this to myself."*

I'm trying my hardest, yet still losing all I hold close to me.
I wanted only to save us, and to never forget our one lasting dream.
So I decided to rise up, and speak out so the world could hear.
I spoke from my heart with pride, yet it sadly all fell upon deaf ears.

So mine was the strength that failed, when I had tried to save the day.
Mine was the heart that was broken, *"because it has sadly always been that way."*
Yours is the hatred that pushes - me that one last step, over and down.
Mine was the voice that failed, as I tried to speak, yet then began to *drown*...

Our Worst Dream

Hard to believe that beyond these eyes we cannot see.
So I have only to laugh at it all just because I cannot breathe.
Here under water just waiting for tomorrow to hurry and pass.
Insanity plus reality, it must equal up to all that I've once had.

Nothing left now, I'm only smoking the stale and redundant ash.
Then as I reach out my hands I begin to feel this world slowly collapse.
I never wanted to hurt anybody *my love* but what now have I left to say?
Just can't believe that all is now over and we're both washed away.

Still here fighting to not admit that our many pointless tries have failed.
So damn numb here, feeling a torment like we've never previously felt.
It was our worst dream and I fear that we sadly are living it today.
Just so fucking hard to believe and you *my love* now have nothing to say.

Then it comes again and again we only want this constant ache to cease.
Here beneath the ocean, it is just so pointless in even trying to breathe.
So *"Now & Always"* we are damned to live on in our worst dream.
Sadly my love we are both dead but *we'll never admit* that we cannot see…

This Knight Persists

Standing here at the peak of a great mountain, so hard to open my eyes.
Looking down at the extensive trail ahead, time again for this knight to rise.
Then once more onward, into the dawn of whatever it is that could lie ahead.
Battle after ruthless battle, another long mile taken with every breath.
And still yet to know the comfort of being home and feeling for once at peace.
To be embraced in the arms of my true love, and to finally know such blissful Grace.
Taking once more, another step to fulfill the vow I've made to you my love.
I am now on my way, to be there at your side in such loving grace.
Now and always I have no time to waste, so on I march towards the light.
I will be with you once again my love, no matter how brutal the strives.
To once again see, far beyond the trails of this damned un-winnable war.
No matter what it takes, we will soon and always be together forevermore.
This Knight persists, for there is nothing powerful enough to stand in my away.
I have felt the sharpness of blades, and the torment of the sands of time.
But once more, it is now that this knight must stand tall and rise.
Then further marching onward towards the end of this war and into her loving arms.
I have made a promise, a pledge that I will honorably keep with persistence.
"I am coming home my love, to be embraced – and to once more hold you in my arms…"

Crossing a Black Cat's Path

So that is my damned luck, now here we go once again.
It has been some time, and once more our paths collide.
And over and over it ensues yet again, so what now to do?
As I come across a black cat, there in the middle of the street.
I have nothing to say and just trying my hardest not to make eye contact.
Then oh yes, it occurs so many times more and more the same.
The relentless bitter luck that I am damned with *forever and a day*.
Crossing a black cat's path, as I take this long walk towards *Faith*.
I guess I can only laugh because this whole world just began to disintegrate.
So that is my damned luck, to be forgotten before I was ever known.
But I guess no one can hear my cries, as I wait here in myself all alone.
Crossing a black cat's path, as it lies there dead in the middle of the road…

Blind I See

In the beginning I held you so close but truly our love was so contrived.
Years and years I fought to not admit it, still I feel broken over the strives.
Numb now I feel nothing, here within my hollow broken heart.
Blind now I see, beyond all the inner torment and pointless scars.

Now frozen waiting, here alone on the dark side of the moon.
Dreams all forsaken, poisoned teardrops falling down over this tomb.
So unfound now, lost in a forgotten place where I know that I should not be.
Then down I fall yet again - feeling so broken, so blind now I see.

Into a last point that was never quite clear, so rickety and distorted.
All the old walls in this house they seem to have been there a thousand years or older.
Then I put my head down, biting my lip in both anger and in shame.
I am so sorry I failed you "*World,*" and again I drift away.

Blind – I hope to see, and yet I know what it looks like here.
Rotten and decaying, within our hearts and every frozen-tear.
My mouth left open, and the spiders spin a web inside my brain.
Blind now I see "my love," that this tormenting pain shall never truly fade…

Mother's Calling

Spinning walls and my mind just can't stop it.
Pain of lock-jaw, and I just can't break it!
Then mother calls, only to ask how I am feeling.
No one answers, because the line at some point must have been cut.

Can no one help me? No – I am damned to fight this War all alone.
Can no one see me, I guess I truly am the forgotten ghost.
I've tried to be there, and yet I was always pushed aside - so far away.
I know mother's calling, yet she never really did hear my screams.

The world it is ending, so someone take my hand and let us fly.
To a better place in existence, far beyond our decaying black sky.
Let's take a deep breath, then choke on all the relentless smoke.
Let's say that we love each other, then try our hardest to hide the lie.

Mother's calling, she wants to know how I've been.
At least mother's trying, to make up for so much lost time.
Mother's crying, as on and on and on and on the phone just rings.
Then sadly mother remembers, *I was nothing more than a fleeting dream...*

Dreaming Alone

I feel I want to breakdown, and just start screaming.
I feel I want to cut now, and just start bleeding.
I think I need to die now, and just let my worries free.
I wish that I could dream now, but never again shall I sleep.

I feel the anger build up, and then it becomes a raging storm.
I can taste as the blood fills up, in my mouth and then I try to swallow.
Down further in sin, and now pain is all that I know in my heart.
Alone here for so many years, just trying not to be torn apart.

Now shattered into pieces, and scattered all over the floor.
Trying my best not to think it, but I cannot deny it anymore.
And on goes the torment, a constant ache that will never pass.
Here in darkness I wait alone, remembering an old dream.
Of when we both loved each other and laughed…

The Darkest Star

What is it truly? The thing that remains hidden behind my heart.
Where are we going? I feel that we've already gone too far.
So what else to say now? Let's just simply smile as we all begin to fade.
Beyond all that has ever been known, and all that shall ever be…

What is it truly? The voice that continues to sing in my soul.
As now our warmth and emotions have all become such a bitter cold.
Where are you going? And tell me why you always had to be alone.
No I cannot stop it! Inside this heart, a frozen black stone.

What are you saying? Oh my God why is your mouth full of blood?!
On now goes all the screaming, and no - we cannot take a short break.
What the hell were you thinking? And don't take that fucking tone with me!
I'm so sorry – I know that you must be in so much pain.
God what was the point truly, in her wishing upon the "*Darkest Star*," known as me?

Hero…

These bones have been broken, now flesh bleeding, weeping tears of pride.
Strength given new meaning, as mercilessly this beaten soldier must rise.
To stand in opposition and take that brutal hit upon the cheek and against the skull.
To be there no matter what, in the warmth of spring or winter's cold…

And oh so painful, as still the hero fights on for this, "Damned World of the Weak."
To be the reluctant scapegoat, so no one else will feel the agony of defeat.
The hero left standing for hours in the rain, no one there to give him thanks.
Yet still the hero fights on – so beaten and broken he still battles every day.

These bones have been broken, when this hero fought to save the day.
Then the world just let him fall and cast him out – so frozen in pain.
Then on and on goes the weeping, because they cannot save themselves this time.
So no matter how much it truly hurts, again this hero must rise…

The Nail That Keeps Me

Fighting hard against the shallow emotions of being a soulless fuck.
Screaming and screaming for years now, and no one ever hears.
No one can see as the blood pours from these eyes like a flood.
Then the room feels with smoke as *"my heart of ash"* slowly comes undone.

Rushing hard against, that frozen stone that sets in my blackened chest.
Here a mile below the deepest ocean, I breathe in deep and wake up dead.
Dead to see that all that I've ever fought for is now only a waste.
A smile as I kick off now, then watch as all memories of her sadly fade.

Above my head now, but still I've got to try and escape this hell.
I loved them all so very much, so I guess I did this to myself.
Oh God no I cannot deny it, the *Awesome* of that *Failure* known as Me.
Then again as I remember our last kiss, I can no longer breathe.

Slamming my head against a door, then anger blinds my aching mind.
This nail it keeps me whole, because it's hammered into the middle of my spine.
Causing a tormenting pain, but at least I know that I'm alive.
As I open my eyes and see, that truly I have died…

A Walk Outside My Mind

Taking a walk, outside my mind - drowning in Voices and the Sands of Time.
Then for some reason, I fall to my knees - so then I laugh as my tongue bleeds.
So where now to go, as my body lies on the ground - both dead and alone.
It's time now to see, what just might be - waiting on the other side.

Taking a walk, outside my mind - it's great now to see that I've gone blind.
Then from across the room, her smile shines - lifting me up to heaven's light.
So I laugh in anger, both Malice and Rage - because truth be-told "I can't be saved."
So taking a nice stroll, out of my mind - dancing so very far and passed the line.

Taking a walk, outside of my head - laughing so hard because I might be dead.
As there on the ground, my body lies - it's sad to think it's already my time.
But then I wake up, so cold on the floor - vomiting out the dirt and ash.
And I am so tired, from taking that long walk - outside of my mind.
But now that I'm back, I can see - that truly we're all blind…

The Space Between

Fall back not to the last words said, *with echoes parading inside your head.*
Then the flesh of this demon becomes so dry, *now* slowly it's flaking off.
And all of the arid casing, once known as this poet's face.
It is all been lost somewhere, and it's never to be replaced.

Push once more unto me, *"the touch of that angel that forever torments me."*
A loud shriek of agony, as both of my eyes begin to boil inside my head.
Then roaring *demonic laughter* creeps over, but still the source is unseen.
It truly feels like I've lost it all, somewhere that I wish to be.

So fall back now, to that hidden place inside, then admit to all the lies.
Laugh so vigorously, in spite of the fact that this is truly the end.
And for so long now, and so very much more must the rhyme continue.
Sadly parading about, in front of their eyes yet forever unseen.
Truly it feels so awkward as now I know I'm lost, *in the space between.*

Decaying Art

God does truly love me, he said so as he ripped out both my eyes.
My love you do truly hate me, I know now as you kiss my lips.
Mother tell me why, as you wash the dried blood off of my face.
But never shall I be clean again, *"forever now and more I bear the disgrace."*

Over so smooth, *as the angels weep diamonds, and they rain down into the skin.*
Thousands of blades of fire, held so high with both glory and pride.
Then the Devil wonders who he truly is, because sadly he's forgotten.
Millions of stars rain from the sky, filling up the deepest oceans.

Snap and a scream, agony frozen as blood gushes from the wound.
Sweetly soft voices now begin to laugh, echoing over the moon.
The teeth begin to grind against bone, but the fact is that it tastes fucking great.
Bloody riddles of now you know but only when you confront the jest.

God I gave it my best, but I was never enough for you my love.
Now sadly our worlds begin to break, soon only a memory shall remain.
On now and forever as the laughter echoes constant beating against my heart.
I know you care not for me my love, I am nothing more to you than decaying art.

My Last Touch

My last touch it felt so numb, then as you pulled on that remaining thread.
I had to scream and laugh as I once again watched myself come undone.
No hope left here in this heart filled with only hatred and rage.
My last touch felt so cold and awkward, as there I lie in my open grave.

Her last words they seemed so dead, null and cold - her beautiful lips.
So frozen as she whispered so softly upon that so damned painful kiss.
Her last thoughts were never shared, *now who's to know what it was for?*
My last hope before I died, was only to see her smile just once more.

My last touch it fell short that day, then for ages upon ages I died.
Never to live in the warmth of the day, never again to feel alive.
Her last wish was for me to be cursed, in the end I guess it came true.
My last touch I ever felt in my life, is when I reached out my hands.
But sadly my love, I just could not save you...

Tearing the Blunt

I can feel them writhing, the rotten maggots on my lips.
Still the burn remains, of when she gave that toxic kiss.
Now over the surface of then the lights begin to dim.
Cold as now we remember that it would be best to just forget.

Open and the whispers sound numb and so very jaded.
Then from behind her eyes, I can see the true meaning.
No we just cannot deny it, as it stares us in the face.
Still I can taste them, the rotten maggots of that grave.

I want to say now, that it was only a joke and we should all laugh.
Then again I remember, all the screams of now no more breath.
I loved it as she held me, and said that I was all she could ever want.
It's like the greatest day ever, until you tear the blunt.

I can smell them, the festering maggots that creep inside my head.
Then as the smoke begins to fill, a scream of frozen breath.
Coughing up chunks now, of meat that looks a bit decayed.
Then as we try to just let it all go, we tear the blunt.
"So we're shit out of luck today..."

Castle in the Sand

Inspiration found that day, upon the golden beach.
A cool breeze of wind, blowing soft through her hair.
So then this mind tries to envision, just how it would feel.
To be the one she loves, beyond this earth and so much more.

The castle in the sand, that is where we could make our home.
To watch over the shores, on and on until the end of time.
She would hold me so close because of that growing cool breeze.
I would love her forever, and forever more as she loves me.

Motivation lost that day, upon the golden sands.
A dark cloud began to loom, and we just did not understand.
Nor shall we ever, *because we are blind* here with sand blown in our eyes.
So as the waves take our castle away, we now have to say goodbye…

Lick My Brain

Push hard with your tongue into my aching brain.
Rub it so gently, till it causes such a delightful pain.
Shove your cold fingers so deep, into both of my eyes.
Lick my brain with your rough tongue, *comfort me with more of your pointless lies.*

Fuck me harder, with your rusted nail so deep inside my heart.
Reach into my lungs, and then eat all of the rotten tar.
Embrace me so softly, as you eat away my flesh.
Bite and tear now at my decaying brain, hopefully soon I'll just forget.

Touch now it so smoothly, the very top of my spine.
Run your tongue across it, in a shock now I scream.
Ride my dick all night my love, until one of us bleeds.
Lick my brain because I know you love that.
Then you just spit out all my memories and walk away…

Playground Terror

Was I never, and always to be, alone in the dark, *"mother save me!"*
As now I can't, and never I could, reach out my love, *"I need you close."*
What was the point, I now don't know, as I sit all alone here, *"so – so cold."*
Tell me now, before you go, please don't hurt me, *"yet still I feel broke."*

I ran one day, to try and get the first look at what's *on the other side.*
I tripped over my shoelaces and fell head first into a lost place in time.
I wanted to be the one, there to save them all from their hurts and pain.
I sadly might have got it in the end, and that might be why I'm insane.

I want to play, yet why always must I be cast out of everybody's game.
I want to fight, but I'm too weak, so then I'm just pushed to the side.
I want to scream, but no one would be there to hear my cries.
I want to kill them all and then laugh at the cold empty playground.

Was I always, and never to know, beyond my mistakes, *"our sad truth."*
As sure as can be, that pain that drives me into the dark, *"so fucking cold."*
What was the point, all the rhetorical nonsense, filling me, *"full of rage?"*
Tell me now, before we go, why won't you, *"just let me play…?"*

These 4 Walls

These four walls cause so much pain.
Smooth upon that lovely voice of when the angel sings.
Hopeless screaming nonsense forever echoing inside my head.
Laughter of the fact that we tried our best but still we're dead.
These four walls remind me of hell.
A tormented reality I can never escape.
No matter how hard I try.
Still now and always shall I never be saved.
These four walls seem to be so broken.
Or maybe it's all just in my head.
And still no matter how hard I try to wake you my love.
I just have to admit to the fact that you are dead.
These four walls, I just wish they would burn.
Then maybe for once I might get a little rest.
Please somebody hurry and destroy these four walls.
That keeps me here locked forever inside of my own head…

Let Me Fall

Please let me fall and just fade away.
Please just let me crawl, down beneath my grave.
A million miles below, into the darkest place in hell.
Let me fall away, and be forever overwhelmed.

Let me fall and just fucking die.
Please ease yourself by erasing your mind.
Now only smiles on blank sheets of white paper.
Of now the fact is that we are beginning to freak..!

Please now let me fall to the other side.
But weep not my love, for I have only died.
A million blades still, stabbing at the back of all my thoughts.
If ever you truly loved me my dear, *"then please just let me fall…"*

Finders Keepers

The finders keep as this loser weeps, all alone there broken on the floor.
A failing want of that nothing that I need, to dig out the thoughts of that whore.
God hold my hand and let us scream, so maybe we won't feel so insane.
Please help me out now, from this old fading emotion that I fear to keep.

The finders lose and the keepers gain, as our failing worlds fill with rage.
A thick lingering smoke, of *"Oh yes"* this is the place where dreams come alive.
This is the final act in this script, but still I have a little more time.
As I dream to hope and I hope to see, far beyond this amusing haze.

The finders hate - for this loser only laughs, as still they try to burn me alive.
But the flames do not hurt me, I only feel the yearning to escape this hell.
I truly did love you once, but maybe it was all just a sad dream.
Of when I held an angel, but her love I could not keep.

The finders die and the losers laugh, because it was sadly all for naught.
Then I begin to feel my soul rot, here now as I wish someone would save me.
So I hide and forever you seek, in your every hope and thought.
Of the fact that still the finders keep and so sadly my love, the losers weep.

Chapter 5

The Shadow Beneath Me.

Battery

Battery keeps it running, pulsating – *"Oh yes"*.
Battery keeps it moving, as she begins to hold her breath.
Between her legs, held so tight and *Oh* so gently she screams.
Battery keeps it running constantly, as she keeps it held between.

Her tongue is writhing, all the way to the tip.
Then she lets out a soft moan, just under her breath.
Of now she is moving her hands down, gently so rough.
Battery keeps it going, so she needs only to enjoy.

Battery is fueling, driving her lusts beyond the point of No Return.
Her eyes roll back, soft laughter behind her moan.
Then right there, *"Oh yes"* battery is fueling her every lovely scream.
Battery keeps it constantly going, the *"little-death"* as she holds it between.

My Punishment

Time to say it mattered, far beyond those fears and pains.
Then you fall on-forth, into and over your every hope to be saved.
Time now for us to let go, and admit that we were once in love.
Then as we try to remember, all those memories fade into dust.

Hope was worth it at one point, then we sadly opened our eyes.
Death was a great joke one day, and everyone laughed but I…
Loss of a great thought, the one that kept all the monsters and demons at bay.
And I guess that was my punishment, to stay here as you walked away.

Time to say we're sorry, even if we didn't commit the crime.
As for so long now, just waiting on another bitter little irony for me to rhyme.
Time to take a deep breath, then exhale all our trivial worries and fears.
As left here for so many ages, these eyes have become as stone.
"So never again shall I shed another tear."

Trust was put to the test once, but the truth is grim indeed.
Love felt so great once upon a time, in this tome in which no one reads.
And it did hurt me so, as there I stood painfully watching you walk away.
So I guess this is my punishment, to be the only blind man that can see...

Breaking the Shame

Of now the lights have gone, numb and dead in me.
Take my hand my love, and guide me to the sea.
Hold my head beneath the waves, until I no longer kick.
Smile now my love as you kiss me, with your wicked lips.

Whisper it into my thoughts, of a dream known only as mine.
Help me break the shame, of being filthy swine.
Push then just a bit harder, and embrace me as you laugh.
I can feel your heart beating on mine, _and I can smell honey on your breath._

Fight now that bastard, he is only a worthless man of fear.
There he waits all day, in that puddle of your bloody tears.
Put your hands together, pray for this soul that is damned.
For here and now I am breaking the shame, of being myself again.

Eating Seeds

I can live with it I guess, knowing she was only a passing dream.
Did ever I have a chance to be saved, "I would love to believe."
OH GOD THE NAILS ARE PULLING THE FLESH BACK!
All is gone now, so the ending must rest with me.

Below now that pool, diving headfirst into a forgotten time.
Did ever I not feel so dead, when she kissed me on my eyes?
OH FUCK THESE DEMONS THAT ARE EATING AWAY AT ME!
Then slowly as here I rot, I become just another seed.

I can live with it I guess, knowing that we've always been dead.
Did ever I truly feel love in my life, "No – not a chance."
OH GOD KILL US NOW OR JUST LET US FADE AWAY!
Our lord God will never help us.
He just spits them out now, _the shells of the seeds…_

Pulling the Pin

And up goes it there, pushing the last nerves beyond repair.
Then down inside her heart, all my twisted logics tearing us apart.
A brutal hit within so loud, so we're pulling the pin just to get out.

A flash and loss of sight, so now I can see the shadow beneath me.
Gone now and nothing remains, as sanity surely eats at me.
No we cannot control the push, of the dying emotion of _hoping to be free._

The pin is pulled, so now it's all up to faith.
We're lost so deep in the woods, we might never be saved.
Now we must only bide our time, to _see it through_ to the end of this day.

And up goes it there, pushing so hard against the grain.
So then we pull the pin, and wait to hear what God has to say.
It's time to release now, and just hope that we might be saved...

The Dying

I am your fucking hatred flowing.
I am the bitter darkness growing.
I am the pointless nonsense knowing.
I am your last chance of hoping to see...

You are just falling so very much unseen.
You are weeping both ash and bloody concrete.
You are now hating this world and this time.
You cannot escape it, the answer behind the rhyme.

I am your fucking hatred exploding.
I am the insane logic still holding.
I am the fear and panic that is flowing.
I am the reason behind all that you seek.

You are the fallen still waiting to fall.
You are the forgotten whim that dwells within sin.
You are now the nonsense that demands to fight.
You are the dying, still waiting for life.

Insect Anticipations

She feels it now beneath the ground, pulsating just below her feet.
She dreams so long for months and weeks, of now she is all alone.
She whispers soft and yet none hear, as on she waits for years and years.
She feels it now beneath the ground, the insects infesting me.

She takes a breath long and deep, and then breathes out the remaining ash.
She remembers a bit of that time spent, when we were both young.
She wanted only to be happy and free, *"no worries or cares."*
She can feel it now and hear it loud, the insects feasting on me.

She took her time and had a drink, as she thought of the past.
God and the Devil are not here today, so she takes my hand and laughs.
She hopes only to see, passed this grim corpse so decayed.
And as she places *"her tongue into my mouth,"* the insects then begin to anticipate.

She feels it now from the ground, the insects crawling up her feet.
A tickle all over her legs so she laughs, and the insects still rise.
She feels them all over and loves it best, *"between her legs and over her breast."*
An anticipation satisfied, as we lie together and let the insects infest.

Lacerations

There is a darkness in this world, in which none can realize.
A place locked deep in the shadows, a place known as our minds.
Fear of the wrong words spoken, but no one was ever right.
Hatred of what it is that we have become, *"Shallow and so Naïve."*

A slap against my cheek, when you say what it is that you said.
I can't believe you feel that way about me, so ominous and so grim.
I gave it all and so very much more, to keep you happy and entertained.
Then again you push me when you say what you say, and then in spite you walk away.

Beaten so hard again, even though I know that I'm all alone.
Thousands of lacerations all over my body, *"a lack of blood and I'm so cold."*
Your hatred is so scarring, my heart just can't take this anymore.
So I rip it out of my own chest, and then smash it against the floor.

There is a darkness in this world, hidden behind all that you see.
Beneath every scar, and dwelling within every tear that is shed.
Lacerations of when you push so hard, with those negative words.
Still I just can't believe what we've become, *"Shallow and so Absurd."*

Derelict

There is no one here standing at my side today.
I guess I'm alone again, and in the smoke I swallow the *fears and shames*.
There is no one here today for me to embrace.
So I guess I'll just wait for tomorrow, *and* on *and* on *and* on I wait...

There is no one truly out there today.
All the streets are empty, this city is now but an empty grave.
Just ghost and memories linger on, of those times of peace.
But no one is out there today, so hollow and the clouds become bleak.

Was there ever truly someone out there?
Someone that cares about all the little things and the value of a good laugh.
Is no one out there, beyond the rainy clouds and stars?
There is no one here today, standing at my side.
It is so very hollow here, this cold dark place inside of your mind.

LeChusa

Damn so cold out here tonight, this walk to try and clear some things.
So damn dark down this street, still I just want to get away.
Then I trip over a mushroom but I keep telling myself it is going to be okay.
Damn so cold out here tonight, this walk to get something straight.

Chills as I try to grasp my jacket tighter, the wind softly begins to moan.
Then a loud terrifying shriek, cold chills run down to my very soul.
In the distance I see something I can't quite make out, but *She* seems to have no face.
Again she screams and moans, and then she said my name…

Now trying to run, as she begins to spread her wings and takes flight.
Running as fast as I can, nowhere to go, "all the doors are locked."
Again she screams my name, and I can feel it like a cold hand around my throat.
As I turn and she reaches her claw out towards me, and then …… …. … ……. … .. … ..
…. …. .. …. .. …….. .. …. … ….. .. …. ….

Counting to Zero

I don't know what to tell you now.
I never wanted it to be this way.
I just can't stop any of this from ending.
So give me a kiss then we'll say goodbye.

No I will not let this be only a cheap mistake.
If we cannot save ourselves then maybe I'll just let us fade.
I never wanted to hurt anybody, damn and I did.
So come on then and just push me, right the hell over the ledge.

You've pained me for ages now, in my hollow heart.
Now here with my head under water, I just gaze up at the stars.
So please just hold me and tell me now that we will both be okay.
Then as quick as you can count to zero, it all just fades away.

This Red Fluid

This red fluid seeping out of all the little cracks in the walls.
I don't know why it reminds me of a time now spent.
This red fluid feels thick and tastes ever so sweet on my tongue.
I don't know why I just laugh here by myself, as I come undone.

This red fluid feels strange as it runs down my face so warm.
Maybe it's because I just got done slamming my head against the floor.
Now so broken and so bitter, in spite it was all just a twisted joke.
Then I cough up this red fluid, which tastes so sour and feels so cold.

This damned head ache, I just wish someone would turn off the lights.
But I am afraid because I know no one's out there, nobody to save me.
From a time now spent and a thought faded for more than an age.
And as this red fluid seeps out of all the cracks in my skull.
It all feels numb and so strange…

Step on a Crack

Push me running, now falling faster.
Timeless wasting, childish laughter.
Hopelessly hopeful, dreams of the light.
Don't forget your prayers, then turn off the lights.

Now catch me if you can, I'll hide and you seek.
You got me on a rant, and I think it's got the best of me.
So stop me if you can, I'll laugh and you'll cry.
Don't step on a crack, and you did and then you died.

Push me faster, round and round and now we fall.
Sing along on this pointless rant, just to free it all.
Hopelessly still hoping, for a chance to see the light.
Don't step on a crack "you did" and now we all will die.

Little Sister Out of Reach

Sweet little sister now out of reach.
Please if you can hear this, then try to find me.
Innocent little sister now out of reach.
What ever can I do to reach you again?

It is dark there, spinning and voices fall numb.
Sound now of that ringing, it tears into your heart.
Screaming in nightmares of what has been done.
Sweet innocent little sister now out of reach.

Terror bleeding of endless screaming.
Little sister is lost and cannot find her way home.
Of monsters eating, tearing and feeding.
Little sister weeps as she sits there alone.

It is dark out there, all the cold and lonely streets.
Please if you can hear this, try to open your eyes and see.
That you can make it out without the bitter agony of defeat.
But I sadly cannot help you now, my little sister – out of reach...

Facing the Day

Facing the day on a bitter lie, but the sad part is that I don't know why.
I've been ripping the flesh off my bones, "now I feel more like me."
I took a chance and said, "*I love you*" God tried his best but had to laugh.
Now facing the day, and trying my hardest to just hold my breath.

Facing up against the world, every time I decide to state my views.
I had a loyal army at my side, but it's not the same nor am I too.
Well there's war to wage, blood that must be paid in full.
So here we go once again, facing the day like fools.

Now facing the day on your bitter lies, the best part is I don't care why.
I've been tearing the flesh off of my body, so I can feel more at home.
I took a chance when you said, "you love me" yet now sadly we're both cold.
Facing the day *on a bitter lie*, searching only for a better question to find.

On a Bitter Lie

On now that push of the "*Not-nothing*" that we said.
Fear of that which keeps us pondering, what might be hiding under our beds?
Ten thousand nails standing in the middle of the road.
Each and every one standing for a pointless committed sin.
And God turns his head in shame of what we have become.
Bitter swine, which wait on and on for the sun to rise again.

Such a bitter sweet, as I drown here in your deceit.
Laughter dripping down and filling all the open cracks on the floor.
And so ever much and more of the tiny whispers that flutter within.
Moving now deeper into love, screaming as we watch the end of our world begin.
On a bitter lie, of that which was once and should *not have ever* touched.
And as we both gaze up at the stars, I know no one gives a fuck.

Tired of reaching when knowing that no one is there.
Echoing of memories, songs of repetitive notions, both hate and fear.
Ten million knives-standing firm in the middle of the winding road.
Then as we trip over and land head first against a blade.
Have to laugh, have to weep, have to go now, time to sleep.
On now that push, *of the said not nothing that gets us through the day.*

Holiday for a Heretic

Looking back and it all just seems like laughter.
Teardrops that fall against the rotten old pages causing such a clatter.
Of dancing echoes that grope so rough over all that stands between.
Must? - And here we go again once more upon this damned road of leaves.

So far out now and once again we head deep into *the thirteen oceans of snow.*
Great to have a little time for myself and yet I'm never alone.
Still in expectation of better prospects and what ever to be now lost.
Truly as my heart has always believed in, the power of an everlasting love.

Reaching back further into this brain made of rotten flesh and tar.
Never as always been seen discreetly hidden behind each frozen scar.
Great to get away every now and then, still I sadly open my eyes to see.
I'm still here locked in myself and never to escape again from this dream.

Looking back over it all, it seems as if it were only laughter and screams.
Confused troubled unforgivable notions hanging onto that last string.
I'm glad to say that I can get away from it all every now and again.
So here once more I shall wait, *beneath this frozen lake of tears she has wept.*

Digging Under the Flesh

Got no fucking time, so here, so here, so here, so here I wait.
Agony felt as I dig beneath the flesh with this fucking rusty blade.
Jaw locked, I CAN'T TAKE THIS SHIT ANY MORE!
So here, so here I wait digging under the flesh, *Oh* what a bore…

Alone now and push it, because I was never meant to be alive.
Fuck I know that you were truly worth it, the selling of my eyes.
Now I cannot reach you, I JUST WANT THIS TO END TODAY!
As here I, as here I wait digging under the flesh to feel how it tastes.

Oh no pressure, FUCK YOU AND ALL THAT YOU STAND FOR!
I never meant that, and yet we both know that *I truly did.*
Please forgive me, I was never meant to be the one to stand in the light.
So here, so here, so here I wait digging under the flesh.
With this fucked up rusted knife.

Loving to Hate Me

Hating the thought of losing you.
As you're loving the thought of misplacing me.
Frantic conniptions bring a twist of the down-broken emotions of pain.
Loving the touch of your beautiful smile.
As you're repulsed every time that I say your name.

You're taking advantage and you've gone too far this time.
As I'm loving the blissful pleasure of being at your side.
Oh Fuck all the metaphoric nothings that bleed from this abstract mind.
Someday we'll learn to live in tranquility, after we open our eyes.
To see clearly all the hidden truths behind the lines.

Fearing the thought of losing you.
As you're so delightfully in the thought of forgetting me.
Hysterical acts of violent tearing at the roots of this bloody brain.
And as *those memories* linger on, I begin hating the thought of loving you.
Because you're so loving the thought of hating me.

This Empty Field

With every awkward step taken, another mile lost.
After every painful breath we intake, we begin to lose another day.
Once again I find myself lost, within this endless haze.
Here so faded as I go tripping through this empty field of mushroom-screams.

Still sanity fades and I fear I can no longer see the shadow beneath me.
Ten million times a day, must we move on into lost hopes of sincerity?
Never again to unearth as now all has been covered by years of mold.
Carved so deep into my forgotten face, our bitter-sweet story untold.

Wandering so awkward, as here I trip in the middle of an empty field.
Both my eyes have been ripped out, so I wait for you on top this hill.
Forever now and just, maybe a little bit of our wretched *inevitable truth*.
Endless and so painfully forgotten, wandering lost without you...

Anguish

It'd be just so much easier to smile as the trigger is pulled.
Getting dizzy as falling down the spiral and now drowning in the pool.
It's felt now all over, every place her fingers have touched.
Agony all over the surface of this shell, so cold and so flushed.

Against the brick wall smashing, blood splattered ever so cruel.
Pure aggressive fits of rage as here still locked inside and don't know what to do.
A jagged blade hidden, then from beneath the rotten flesh it's pulled.
Anguish felt all over both within and out of this mind so cold.

It'd be just so much easier to *wave goodbye* as we step over the ledge.
Then down all goes and is never to be seen ever again.
As felt so brutal all over, agony in this heart because now she hates me.
Anguish has truly become my life, as here I just laugh with my insanity.

Water

The ghosts have come and are ready to play.
The lights are off and the music fades.
Tomorrow comes, as today is now but a dream.
The ghosts now lead the path, so far beyond all that we see.

Now the water is rising over our heads.
The snow is freezing as it dances with our breath.
In fear now we are drowning, at the bottom of this endless pool.
Here beneath the water, realizing the dream as now darkness is pulled.

The ghosts have all wept and then said goodnight.
These eyes can see nothing now because they are blind.
Tomorrow comes and once again it fades away.
The water is freezing, "as so numb now, we no longer feel pain."

Advent Failure

And in the flame it can be seen, misled afar into forgotten seams.
Felt vicious vindictive words of how that day, it was lost between.
Then as sanity commenced to telling me that I am insane.
Just have to laugh so hard because again I'm only fighting me.

Too far to go, so I'll wake you when we arrive.
You look so peaceful when you sleep *and* softly sigh.
Then endless hysterical screaming and I just can't see the reason.
I don't know why it always ends this way, so silent in the night.

And in the flame it can be seen, misled memories yet to fade.
Felt so violent, the heartrending fact that this soul can't no longer keep.
Then as the dogs begin to howl, out far deep in the woods.
Just have to laugh because we've gone too far, and still have much to go.

So put yourself in my shoes, as here I stand so deep in yours.
Wandering far into the dark, hoping someday we might be found.
Then as we try to say it's all okay, still this pain knows no bounds.
"These rusty nails - this flesh it peels - away again and I have failed..."

You Can't Save Me

You can't save me from what I've become, hollow and so dead.
You can't stop me from loading this gun, with all my futile sins.
You can't deny me any longer, I am now the monster you fear.
You can't save me today my love, *"and yes I know you don't care."*

You've always hated me, I guess because I've always loved you.
You've never cared for me, not the way that I've cared for you.
You've only wanted me, to just let go and fucking fall away.
You've always just laughed every time, *and I just wish to see tomorrow stay.*

You can't protect me anymore, I am already dead in my grave.
You can't hold me close now any more, *all the butterflies have flown away.*
You can't forget me now, as I stir in your every last dream.
You can't deny what I have become, *"and no my love you cannot save me."*

The Grass Of Blades

Faded lost for once again, those hours of ages now sadly spent.
As falling harder against – the memories grow and begin to decay.
And once again I trip, into the endless fields, *"of the tiny beautiful blades of grass."*
Still beating myself over the thoughts of what it was we had said in the past.

On now and over, still dragging my tired body over every hill I may encounter.
Laughing so many years now, for I have yet to see an end to the horizon.
Hills upon hills I'm climbing, then head first falling over my own feet.
Plummeting down, then just have to scream, endless through all the pain.

Pulling myself on now further, pushing aside the tiny little blades of grass.
Forgetting what it was that made me love you, *"as remembering it's all now ash."*
And *oh* such a sadistic pain, felt now at the bottoms of both my feet.
Blood filling my worn-down shoes, *"as I journey over these hills an eternity."*

Faded lost for now and always, fighting to regain what it was that I once had.
As troubled now like once and before, hiding there behind that open door.
For only that reason, as when she held me so close until all my fears began to fade.
As so here I go on now tripping, over the tiny beautiful blades of grass.
The eternal fields - of *"the grass of blades…"*

Virus Called Hope

Feeling now so fucking sick, sour chunks rising in my throat.
God hold me now because I think this is it, and damn it's getting cold!
Just can't think now, too many fucking demons on my mind.
You reach out but cannot save me, so bitter *"yes"* it must be the lime.

Can't take the nonsense, the sleepy drug is making my head spin.
All the blood rushing out of my body, can't believe it's happening again!
Razors shining so warm now beneath my tongue and behind my words.
I swallow, then frantic laughter, as all now seems so fucking absurd.

Oh God! And once again I can feel the sour chunks begin to rise.
I don't want to see this go on anymore, so I guess I'll close my eyes.
Please somebody save me, "I don't know what the hell is going on."
It feels like I'm dying, God please infect me with your virus called hope.

The Wooden Box

Oh so many years, now this wooden box has become aged and moldy.
All the contents have sadly become but only dust and ash.
This wooden box can't keep it safe forever.
Hidden so far away, just beneath her beautiful flesh.

This wooden box, holding so many secrets – "yet I won't tell."
All hopes of ever reaching the end of the platinum rainbow.
It's gone now and everything has become such an awful trip.
No we cannot touch the picture now, feels like the paint is still wet.

Oh get me out! As now for so many years here screaming to be free.
The wooden box, it's holding something more than we'd ever wish to know.
Locked deep where no one can find it, lost forgotten in a sad dream.
And again I awake alone, and still the inside of this wooden box is all I see.

Watching You Run Away

Shaky finger tips pressing deeper into the open wound.
Broken glass and dirt felt inside, remains of a tattered youth.
As now so resistant in every shitty bitter word you seem to spew.
The fingers reach now the injured bones, felt so neglected and abused.

Forgiven naught the forsaken thoughts of the end and it equals dismay.
Blood rushing from the jagged open wound in the middle of this chest.
Then as I watch you run away, just have to say that it's for the best.
Hesitant words spoken, then so sorry for what it was that I did…

Sweet and so innocent, her tongue resting beneath mine.
Destroyed notions of what was once, and now only a fading echo through time.
Untaken dire hopes now weeping, because the pain is too much today.
So in the end I have to say it's for the best, *just watching you run away.*

Growing into Death

One page left then another chapter in life becomes burnt.
As all eyes gaze upon me I feel as if I'll never truly learn.
For so very much, of those damned emotions that bring forth only pain.
That lovely sting as I remember, that we are both utterly insane.

As you stare back at me in my eyes through the mirror.
Just can't help but tell that your face reminds me a bit of my own.
An old man soon to fade away, into dreams of something much more.
Just one more page to conquer, one last step and then we're home.

Feels like I might finally be growing into my own death.
Life becomes cold now, a lingering chill on my tired breath.
Seems so stagnate still as all my echoing words reflect nothing of me.
Just so fucking sad that I've grown into my death.
Then the Devil said he wasn't ready for me...

Leprosy

Seems as if I can no longer recognize the shadow beneath me.
This body is shattered all over, this shell can no longer keep me.
No it cannot be - no they cannot see all the truths that lead to the end.
No they never touch me, no they never have seemed to care.

Can no one reach me, can no one hear all my faint screams.
So will no one save me, can no one take me there to the peek.
Then as I take in all of my surroundings I realize the grim tragedy.
That no one can help me, no one shall touch this surface again.

I feel like a broken vessel, cracked in two and now discarded.
Like a cancer it eats at me, so I cover myself to keep it from spreading.
It truly seems as if I can no longer identify this shadow beneath me.
No one will ever save me, guess I'm just a fucking leper.

Seems as if there would be a greater end to this nonsense.
But again you search for a deeper meaning that does not exist.
The sad fact is that I'm falling apart here and now as we speak.
I just feel so alone sometimes in this crowded world I cannot reach.

Chapter *6*

Standard Insanity.

Little Pretty Pill

As falling down and gazing up, watching the stars being pulled away.
Are we ready now, to admit my love, never shall tomorrow be saved.
So pretty yes, that gentle touch felt so shallow in my empty eyes.
It gets just so hard to swallow, as watching our beautiful star lights die.

These hands reaching out, trying to get a grip on the hanging threads.
Such *demonic laughter* begins to seep out, as we come undone once again.
Now we have to scream, *have to cry*, need to breathe yet now all is blind.
Just waiting for reason, as now falling so much deeper within the page.

Then again it all shocks me, to feel now so numb and jaded.
As holding the remains of the pills, and remembering how it tasted.
Rotten of the breath you spew, over your sick demented words.
And after all the little pretty pills we have taken, you'd think we would learn.

The Smoke Invades Me

The smoke invades, as I sit back and watch the coals burn *with-inside* me.
Behind my tired eyes, *can God see* the true end that I've chosen to let be?
Felt so cruel and twisted, as only rust rises up then all across the floor.
Painted *forever and never* to fade, this picture of a love that is no more.

The smoke invades, as night begins to blister beneath this tattered shell.
Then as my eyes open so painful in front of this stained mirror.
Still I just have no fucking clue, as to why I keep doing this to myself.

Am I but only a nonentity, hoping to see the light beyond the cloud?
Am I truly just a freak, forever *the neglected child* our world has cast out?
And does that mean you are the one, that waits behind the open door?
As I feel the smoke invading me, I wish to care for never-more.

The *smoke it is enduring,* as is *all the bitter thoughts* that remind me of you.
So I laugh as I feel my sanity leaving me, still don't know what to do.
So I guess I'll just sit here, waiting for our beautiful sun to rise.
And as I let the smoke invade me, just need now to close my eyes.

" With a smile, all gently now drifts away..."

It Was Her Song

Maybe it was our failing song, those questions unforgivable.
Maybe I held on too long, then *Love* commenced to taking it all away.
Hopeless now, I've given up and this world now seems just so odd.
And on and on through all these continual aches, still *we sadly sing along.*

So in the end were we not meant to hold each other forever and more?
It was our song, resonating for years as *all the memories continue to pour.*
For now these dead-eyes cannot see the truth that waits just beneath.
I guess it was her song, which repeats unending now in my head.
As still to this very day the thought of her touch, silently my soul it condemns.

Precious

"We are so precious now – can't you see....?"
As we pull together all the lose ends known forever as – you and me.
So time has come and lain its hands over the surface of us.
A child laughs in the distance, yet today we cannot reach.
We are so precious, connected eternal in deadication and love.
"We are forever so precious, the one being known as the two of us..."

It's Killing You

Please open your eyes, open your eyes to see...
Please don't let me go, don't let me go and fade so weak.
Remember me now, hold the blade and speak my name.
Please kill me now, my love just kill me now today...

It's killing you, the killing of me as on the pain still goes.
It's killing you, as you're killing me, left now so – so cold.
It's hurting you, because you're hurting me as you walk away.
Please just let me fall, God let me fall and release some shame...

Please open your eyes, just open your eyes so maybe you can see...
Please tell me that you're still alive, as you begin killing me.
Forget me please, just say that it's all for a reason much greater.
It's killing you, while it's killing me, the memories of our laughter...

Now the Child Sees

So now the child can see, *"Not quite a fuck up today..?"*
And again the world it blames me, for all its uninhibited mistakes.
Nothing now can save us, mankind is failing before our very eyes.
So now the child sees, what was once hidden behind the truthful lie.

So used up here and now, damaged goods and cast away.
Into the gutter, that is where mother found her son today.
Such a sinful bliss felt as the purple velvet ropes begin to tighten.
Hard to breathe with the air so cold, then from these lungs bleeds fire.

So now this child can see, *"Not quite what our God has made of me."*
And again the world burns and I'm left all alone in space.
Nothing to comfort me through the ages, *only the darkness of my mistakes.*
So now the child sees, beyond the truthful lies, now destroying faith...

Nerve Dead

This world that lies hidden behind my twisting eyes.
It holds a resonating truth my heart will forever despise.
A God damned memory I just wish our lord would forsake.
And as it all keeps on spinning, I can feel now nothing in me.

Nerve Dead I guess, can't even feel the blade pushing beneath the flesh.
Still the wound bleeds, rushing hard, now seems you like that best.
As the lesions gush, overflowing and draining into the endless pit.
And it causes such a fit, knowing I no longer feel a damned little bit.

The words wait hidden, behind these eyes that see only fire and rage.
Reality and fantasy have become just so numb, life now seems so strange. .
I just wish I could hide it, still I wish I could deny it, yet it is the same.
I must be nerve dead, because as you killed me, *I didn't even feel a thing.*

Fuck The System

Walking into a corrupted temple, listing to the squeal of each filthy swine.
Realizing now just how senseless it is, the preaching of hope beyond dismay.
To the slaughter now my loves, let us follow on-forth into the grinder.
So scream now mother and father, the end has come and now it is time.

Fuck the system and all it has ever stood for, honor, justice, truth and faith.
Fuck this world, let us watch as it burns, here beneath our own smoldering feet.
Damn all the bitter questions that hang there on the tips of their hearts.
Fuck it all and so we laugh, as we begin now tearing each other apart.

Walking into a decaying old courthouse, but the jury was out today.
Still I stand here judged, as all still push their evil eyes upon me.
Piercing cold as her ghost places its dead fingers against my lips.
So I scream so I dream, as on and on, "I just want this now to fucking end!"

Fuck the system and all that makes up each connected branch and root.
Fuck the God that spent all its precious time creating a waste like you.
Damn it all, the bottomless sea and this dream of a life that just won't end.
Fuck you all and every second of every pointless day in which we have spent.

At War With Me

So sad to say, that these failing souls we just cannot reach.
Can never the end of justice come forth and present itself to me?
We've been there yes, so many times these hearts smashed to the core.
Then as the stammering voices push on, it's time again for another war.

Then from these rusted eyes, sadly now we just cannot see.
Agony felt as their hands of thorns tear inside, taking all of me.
Into the dark, where none will search, none shall ever find a thing.
Here in this eternal dark pit, somewhere, in someone's fucked up brain.

"Then as I stand beside myself in misery, we just have to laugh, have to scream!"
Taking that inevitable hit, felt deep in the middle of this absurd dream.
Where now can we go, to find maybe just a ray of light in this dark?
So what to say as I stand beside myself, just have to cry, have to bleed.
But at least I know I'm never alone, while at war with me...

Wish You Could See...

Maybe now as the haze begins to subside, try my love to open your eyes.
Please tell me something, just so I can hear your gorgeous voice again.
And as the sun lies to sleep, I just know now that this is the end...

Maybe someday, tomorrow might not feel so dead.
Hopefully as I rummage through all the ashes, I might find myself once again.
Beneath the pile of pages, here scattered across this cold floor.
Then as I manage to feel something, it's raped away again and I am no more.

I wish that you could see, what it is that I have become.
I'm no longer the child you knew, yet I am still the forgotten one.
I wish that you could see, so maybe you should try opening your eyes.
And again I must remember, the once hidden truthful lie...

Maybe now as the pain begins to subside, try my love, just open your eyes.
Please say something now, just so I can know that you are still okay.
I just wish that you could see, but the life in your eyes my love, it sadly fades...

"Still I wish you could see."

Can I Be Forgiven?

Then as I tried to reach it, God laughed as he took it all away.
So I fell face first against the loose gravel, now bleeding and in pain.
Rage felt with bitter hostilities, flesh torn and bone exposed.
Rapidly the tears are rushing from these eyes, that see our true end...

Can I be forgiven, for all the negative things I've said over the years?
Can I just let go and fall now, behind the drapes - so dark in fear?
When will you just free me, and let my heart find some rest?
Can ever I truly be forgiven, for all the evil deeds I did commit?

Then as I tried to explain, that it was all for reasons I could not say.
The Devil just had to weep, because he looked in mirror *and* saw my face.
Hatred - still it is swelling, deep here within this heart of burning coals.
Please God erase or forgive me, so I no longer have to be alone...

All That I Lost

Spent all night long in dreams, trying to stop this world from ending.
Then I awoke to realize, that everything including myself is gone.
I wish to weep now, but no one will ever again help me to rise.
I spent all nightmare long trying to save them, *then I sadly opened my eyes.*

To the end of all chance, so maybe the universe will just let go.
Again on another rant, onward tripping deep beneath the snow.
Here in this *desert of salt*, are there any other colors left but black and white?
So to think that it is truly over, and I guess nobody at all survived.

The *Darkness* screaming as *Life* is left bleeding, so alone and in rage.
To think that it's already ended and still I had much more to say.
Of all that I've lost over these long years, what would I wish to regain?
Maybe just someday, I might get the chance to see.
Out of all that I've ever lost, the one thing I need now is "*Me…*"

Opening An Umbrella Indoors

Into the slipping - tripping, endless amounts of words pushing ahead.
Must be bad luck, all these taking - breaking lies of the never it was.
So push me falling, as slapping my cheek until you draw blood.
Just say it clearly - as it begins tearing, "*Lord God, what have we done?*"

Shrieking endless - fears of the pain, taken to the beginning *and* left astray.
Where has the Devil gone now, and what did she say?
Reach into my heart now please, and keep whatever you can take.
This must just be bad luck - at least that's what the broken mirrors say.

Just can't bear to go on now, so leave me where ever it is I drop.
Bleed it out - the blistering sounds, of logic broken upon our lies.
Take it far passed the beginning to see, that we are all truly blind.
With open umbrellas indoors, to keep dry in this sad eternal rain.
Must just be bad luck, at least that's what I keep telling myself.
Just gotta hold on - gotta hold on because here we are now.
Right where it all begins...

Tool

For that *"Love"* in my youth, in which I could not save.
For all the turmoil that fills, this bottomless grave.
For all the bastards and whores that say it's too dark.
For all the pointless blood, beneath the shallow scars.

Then given back to me, yet I chose not to see.
Then raped again so brutal, endless - *"all the screams."*
Then misled once more, down that hall and towards the back.
Then when the tool was lost, we knew *it* would never be fixed...

The Zombie's Touch

The rotten zombie eyes open, yet the wooden box is all it can see.
So in one swift stroke the box is broken, once more this zombie is free.
Free to rise again, here in this vast field of forgotten names.
As the zombie begins to moan, it steps out of its muddy grave.

What now has summoned, the zombie searches through the dark.
In hopes to find, of that nothing known forever and soon fade.
What has called forth the zombie to rise again, on this particular day?
The zombie finds nothing, no one, only death in the house of the dead.

So peaceful here, in a place where there is sadly now no more life.
It is so dark out tonight, because the moon is gone so no more light.
But not to care, as still the questions linger on and on and on.
What called this zombie forth, "why now must I rise?"

The zombie's touch, it cannot feel all the changes of the times.
As the moon weeps acid down, into the idea of when light was real.
The zombie's touch, it cannot reach, for life has become so dead.
Yet still this zombie wakes, wondering if it was all only in its head.

Screams of bitter madness, for what was it that made me exist.
Now only the walking dead, still I hope fate will set me free.
The zombie's touch can no longer feel, its rotten eyes cannot see.
Once more now this zombie lies to rest, *on top a hill – beneath a tall tree.*

Still Can't Reach

Sweet voices calling out but where was my mind today?
Still I can't reach, God I need a bit more faith.
Please get me through, "I'm gonna require some help this time."
Still I know not what to say, so I stay here waiting behind the line.

Beautiful angels singing, verses that echo forever in my heart.
God what can I do, to keep me from tearing myself apart?
Still I wish that I could save them all, from the ending yet to be.
But it seems that no matter how hard I try, "still can't reach…"

Timeless hoping, for an outcome that can change the world.
God hold me close, as we all fall tumbling through the void.
Hatred rises, as the sweet voices regrettably begin to fade.
Still I can't reach the "happy ending," _Oh God I need some faith…_

Inside the Gray-Stone

The child lies there waiting, forever and still always to be alone.
Dark and cold there in the hoping, that God might someday care.
Dreams of a better knowing, and still all has ended just the same.
So bitter - _the sour thoughts_ - of now you must admit the mistake.

The child lies awake, years upon years in the blistering cold.
For there is no sun left to warm and ease the child's tattered soul.
So to be now, for that which must never rise to the peak.
Yet still the child hopes and knows now, that this time he's just too weak.

The child lies alone sleeping, dreaming that someday joy might be felt.
But again the child feels only, the pain of those freezing rusted nails.
Digging under, in hopes that we might escape this failing dream.
So again the child lies _awake in the womb_, knowing it shall never be free.

The child screams there hysterical, because it sadly feels only pain.
In this bitter cold prison, of the flesh that our _mother and God_ gave.
Forever and ever and ever some more the child weeps all alone.
Asleep and yet never to rest, inside the gray stone...

Day-Dreaming

I saw *Michael* today, standing at the end of the hall.
I asked him how he has been over the years.
It felt like decades, an age spent since we had last met before.
Michael said he was great, just moving forward as always...
Through all the compilations, of times when we were brothers.
Ready to fight and make sure that we helped out the weak.
I saw *Michael* today, just standing there with a smile on his face.

I asked *Michael* pointless questions, just happy we met again.
Just like all the times before, laughter and poetic nonsense.
To pass our time, through all the pains of this world in which we live.
Michael told me so many things, it all gave me strength to get passed today.
With a smile, compressed against all the rhythmic changes of the times.
I was just so glad I got to see my old brother, after so many years.
Just standing there with a smile, filling the room with cheer.

I saw *Michael* today, he was the same as I remembered from our youth.
Michael had a few things to say, so he spoke clear and unyielding.
I knew not what else to ask him, I only wanted our friendship to last.
Through all the great times and throughout all the bad.
Now for some reason I begin to feel all the grace fleeting.
Michael told me to open my eyes, "so I guess I was only day dreaming."
"For our fallen brother..."

Our Little Secret

Time once more to let, then watch as our flesh becomes as weak as paper.
Time again to forget, because this face never held any true clarities.
Time now to speak, if only our God would allow us the correct words.
Time then to end, for there is no chance of ever gaining the happy ending.

So this is our little secret, of the thing we must never tell.
An unending complication binding our souls to a bitter hell.
As now so weak, we can no longer open our eyes.
To see it clear, of all beyond our fears, true now that nobody won.

Time once again to let, and weep as we all come undone.
Time now to just reach, but this memory did never exist.
Time then to just let go, scream as we wake falling out of bed.
Time to forget our little secret, of the truth we sadly lost at the end.

Platinum Eyes

Platinum eyes reaching into my soul.
Tearing out the demented cancer known as all of my being.
Tried to reach but felt so cold, falling into a place unseen.
With dancing star lights, pulsating just beneath the surface.
Golden memories, sadly now with the times it fades.

Platinum eyes seeping within my heart.
Proving how truly counterfeit their smiles can be.
As here beyond the darkness it all falls, now never again to be at ease.
With hopes of gaining, as all still seems so pail and weak.
Strength begins to leave this body, a thousand miles below the sea.

Faded emotions dancing numb within this mind.
Feasting on the festering cancer that reminds me we're out of time.
Just so cold now and lonely, as I can feel them pressing all against me.
The platinum eyes that see only the sights of the forever unseen.
Held so far within, and taking all that was ever meant to be.

An Ocean Of Tears

Why today must I be so far out, where no one can see?
Why can no one feel me, as all my life I have tried to reach?
To touch the truth that dances behind the stitch.
God help me through this nightmare, so maybe I can *find some rest*.

For now that turmoil, the approaching notions of dismay.
All alone out here, where not even our loving God can see.
Sinking below, so cold as all the echoing star-lights softly sing.
Why must it be this way, so oddly cold as I sink beneath?

In this ocean of tears, here where no one else exists.
It seems so strange to me, the waves of emotions behind my breath.
As gasping so brutal, trying to keep myself from sinking below.
I've tried my very best, but in the end I just can't let it go.

Why – *Oh* why is it that I'm just so far out today?
Lost alone again, where my dreams become realities.
Malicious to the core, out here sinking below the twisted waves.
Drowning in *an ocean of tears*, which seem red and always ends in pain...

On My Throne

The epitome of all that lies bitter at the wake.
Down below the shallow thought of lust as it takes.
Beyond fear, of when she said she was truly alive.
I assume now we are ready, to see tomorrow's light.

Upon the moon I trip, forever I've felt so sick.
In the sky we die, as we open our eyes.

The embodiment of all that waits kneeling upon the broken glass.
Left aside and unaware as our loving memories now relapse.
Into the broken pool of the day we knew we were alive.
I suppose now we are ready, to let go and feel the light.

As upon the moon we trip, in this mind it's felt so sick.
Left beyond our great blue sky, so on my throne is just I...

Questions upon endless questions of that what's taken.
Down below the anguish, suffering as we hold it between.
Now further than we have ever thought, so very miserably lost.
I hope we for once see the light, after we close our eyes.

Then upon the moon I trip, drowning in my gushing blood so thick.
Knowing soon I must die, as upon this throne is only I...

Deranged

And I'll just dream away, sleep again for another day.
Watch as life just slips away, weep again just fade away.
And then you laugh at me, and say the shit that you always say.
"Turn around just walk away..!"
So I'll just laugh at you, and say the shit that I always say.
"Dream again just fade away..!"

Yes my dear we are deranged, lost again – it seems so strange.
Then I'll watch you fade, forever gone – just a memory.
"Taken far where I'll never see!"

So I'll just dream away, sleep again for another day.
Laugh as life just slips away, weep for love but you'll never stay!
Yes – my love we are deranged, just close our eyes and fade away...

Motor Grip

Blood pulled down dripping off the blade.
Blood pooled in the back, rising every day.
The moon holds us gently, now we say this is it.
Then eyes opened to the truth which we'll never get.

As poison pulled down to the edge of this spine.
The demons keep on howling, deep within this mind.
For all of, and none set – the deep breath of time.
As once said, hurt again – at the end of the line.

Blood pulled down off the monsters fang.
Blood pools in the back, rising every day.
The gears are constant moving, taking us all home.
The answers are hidden, just beneath the stone.

As passion was once the meaning, now all is torn away.
This face once was worshiped, but now has been erased.
The motor keeps it running, gripped tight to the bone.
The eyes open to see, in hell we're never alone.

High Noon

A dire query brought forth upon our doom.
Child dreams can see now only our end.
The purple, reasons upon endless reasons of our pain.
We've reached noon, now we step over and away.

Upon the stars, millions of miles outside our universe.
Where maybe someday our dreams could thrive.
We've reached the prime of now it is too late.
You've seen the end, and you just couldn't wait.

Upon a dire query brought forth to confirm our doom.
The children of the world, awake at high noon.
Of soon this will all just pass, faded where none shall see.
We've reach the conclusion of our little story.
Now smile and know this was all but a dream...

She Said Go Deeper

She said go deeper, into my mind where no one can see.
She said to let go, then fall away into forgotten dreams.
She said I was the greatest, of all the demons she did encounter.
She said go deeper, into our pointless eternal nightmare.

For once was the meaning, now darkness is all that's left.
Hatred has become so majestic, as was our one lasting kiss.
She said I was a fighter, someone known as brave.
For once more I must let go, and admit it was all a mistake.

She said go deeper, into the shadows of my perverse mind.
She said to fight the war, and to just give it time.
She said I was an angel, as she held me so close.
She said to cut deeper, until I hit my tattered soul.

For again now is the calling, towards the middle into the back.
Hatred has its hold again, so now it's too late to react.
She said I was a winner, although I've lost all within.
So again once more I must go deeper, just as she had once said...

The Cockroach

Just an insect, absent in the light of my own shames.
I live in the darkness, thriving on our world's *bold and yet valid* mistakes.
Unopened to the back, when was once our true reflection?
Now dire in the gamble, of which was so - *yet cannot* control.
So timid and coy, of all that could be grasped by this pointless insect.

Just a cockroach, hidden in the dark where no eyes can reach.
Afraid of light, which illuminates on that I wish not ever to see.
Of that putrid face, our God has now sadly forgotten.
That to be in shame, just a worthless wretched shell of a demon.
Beyond the void, in regrets and blame, just now an insect *beneath the rain.*

I am the cockroach, an unwelcome pest you wish to destroy.
The unheard of violence, hidden in the darkness of these endless voids.
Never to be honored, only a nuisance you wish to discard.
Left so dire in the gamble, but it's too late to try again.
Just an insect, the cockroach wearing human skin...

Mother Vanishes

I can see *the outline of mother* but now it evaporates like a cloud of smoke.
Into nothing, held firm against all that binds this soul to the truth.
Mother was there once but now it's just a photo in the album.
Between two pages, lost but never forgotten.

The ghosts are whispering the particulars of this situation.
Above all, this is the grim truth we never wanted – to let be.
Mother was there once waiting for tomorrow.
But all of that has vanished, gone now where none can see.

Mother was happy that day, when I first opened my eyes.
This enduring smoke fills the room but shall soon subside.
I can see now that this is the reality I did never want to admit.
As the ghosts reach within, my memories of mother vanish once again.

Mother is gone now, so I'm left in darkness and in fear.
Please somebody save me, I wish only to escape.
Get me out of this twisted dark nightmare and let me breathe!
I want mother back now, so I vanish too, to that place unseen...

Be Careful What You Wish

Be careful what you wish, for it may come to pass.
Laugh my love as I burn, and for you I shall become only ash.
Lost below the foundation, gone now because it was all taken.
To the north dream, as you hold so dear our perverse pains.

Disregarded once at the wake, as Day became but a futile delusion.
Then we were stuck there at the conclusion, afraid to take the next step.
Be careful what you wish my love, for fate has a sick sense of humor in deed.
And for only you my love shall I burn away into ash and eternal nothingness.

Be careful what you wish my love, but then you just turn away.
You've wanted nothing more than to see this soul begin to fade.
It was all taken at the wake, but none ever have seen the light.
You my love have wished us to an everlasting darkness.
So I smile, as I wish this all would just come to an end...

"Papers…"

Millions are towering over head, stacked high in this bottomless hourglass.
Pages upon endless papers that flutter on throughout the night.
Speaking great principles, as filling my head with insane nonsense.
Broken wrath detained, for three lines now stand incorrect.
Contract upon endless contracts leading on and on until death.

As is it filling, the ink that bleeds from these endless paper sheets.
Can you recollect *my God?* Or is it us the world that has gone blind.
To the fact of the torment that pushes from within.
But we cannot speak what we feel, only sign both front and back…
Upon these endless papers and papers between each breath.

Such an annoyance that stands there firm and unaffected.
As these tired lives wish only to live on in peace.
Still these pages fluttering so frantic inside my brain.
It all made sense once, but now a growing tornado we like to call rage.
Then when all is said and done, it was all but just another page.

So passion is the only thing left that connects me to humanity.
Endless hysterical laughter as I realize this is but another *"Standard Insanity."*
It pushes so hard against, but it is an evil we cannot battle.
So we're forced to play along, *"just sign your name, both front and back."*
Papers upon endless papers, leading on – from birth until death…

Chapter 7

Burning the Remains.

Waiting Between

Can't stand to be this way anymore, eyes gazing up as I lie on the floor.
Smoke bleeding softly from the jagged open wound in my throat.
For now life seems so precious, as so viciously it is taken away.
Still can't stand to be where I am, alone on the floor waiting between.

I've reached out there, and felt nothing in this endless dead space.
I have felt pain before, but as like everything else it all just fades.
At the wayside, that predictable gutter in which I always seem to land.
Here I find myself waiting between, tripping onward upon another rant.

Can't bare to be this way anymore, jaw locked as I weep on the floor.
It hurts so terrific, as the platinum sands bleed from my eyes.
It seems so lost out here, this cold space not even our God can see.
For all my life just wanting to let go, as here I'm lost waiting between.

As Our World Decays

I never did understand, why I smiled as the atom bomb fell.
I never did understand, why I ended up pushing us into hell.
It always felt so awesome, as the ghosts ripped away my flesh.
I never understood why you smiled, as you let out your last breath.

For now the entirety of our humanity seems so utterly absurd.
As our world decays, what is it truly that we have learned?
I never wanted "to hurt you my love" now what is it that I can say?
I never understood why you said nothing, as I walked away.

Here in the hopes that there might be light found beyond the darkness.
Why is it that this laughter just continues rising up *and* over all our pains?
Why didn't you desire me to be around, as the great floods began?
All I've ever wanted, was to be at peace and to maybe find some grace.

"I just never understood why we must laugh, as our world decays..."

The Acid Floods

At one end broken, for lies we never shared.
Aside the twisted nonsense, blistering within this mind.
Head full of rotten candy, it sounds like a delicious scream.
Such a soothing drape pulled over, as I lie awake in this dream.

The acid is flooding, my twisted pain-filled mind.
And I feel I cannot control it, the dragon beneath the sand.
And I fear I cannot hold it, the demon with distorted skin.
Just wish my mind to free it, "Jesus save me from myself."

The mushrooms are growing, soon they will eat me alive.
So I drink the clouds to calm me, then all reason drifts aside.
As I hold these broken shards, that was once my forgotten face.
I think I'm gonna lose it soon, so will you come follow me?

At one end broken, the truth of a lie we never shared.
Beside myself with the pure bliss of lunacy.
Corroding within this heart, now bleeding out despair.
For now God is weeping, cradled in mother's arms.
As the acid floods, "*now has taken over,*" *the Devil smiles because we are one.*

Colliding Dreams

Between two lines seen at the edge of the gate.
Another season gone, as the razor separates.
Dedication fueled on pride, while still this heart bleeds.
A million miles taken, and still an eternity unseen.

When suddenly came a tide that pushed forth a notion of change.
Somehow our dreams collided, and brought on an ominous feel.
This flesh became weak, and began to shatter into dust.
Now these bones are all that remain, and soon to be burnt.

Between two lines, that is where God took our faith.
Sugar beneath the tongue, laughter over the pains.
Another season gone, a winter of eternal hell.
But once when our dreams collided, we truly felt like ourselves.

A Slave No More

Haunted still by the phantom memories which linger on within.
Do I remain now as a ghost, too predictable for you to embrace?
But I believe I stand enlightened at this moment in time.
We have reached the end, "I am a slave no more…"

Fed up with this pitiful game the world tries to play.
As on and on they push, but was it ever worth the pain?
I fear it doesn't matter any longer, we have now only to die.
Then fade away into forgotten notes, hidden behind the lines.

So was it not to be, felt then as only another futile scream?
For I am that, which all the other hidden monsters hate.
Still haunted by the past, and waiting for it to all just fade.
Here waiting at the end of the line, "I am no longer a slave."

Here so demented, as the pressure builds stronger inside.
I'm fed up with all this shit, so please God just ease my mind…
But I do believe I stand tolerant at this junction in time.
For I am no longer yours to control, not now or ever.
So please God take me today – "I am a slave no more…"

False Was Our Love

So the emotions come, then again pass away.
My heart has died, so what have you to say?
The dream was great, but then we awoke.
Upon the leaves that lie above the stones…

So the hurt was constant, felt between our laughs.
Bitter looks across the room, *then we say nothing back…*
And for years goes the bleeding, this heart just cannot take.
Of all the false emotions, lying below the slate.

Where was once then the torment, now but an outline of chalk?
The voices kept it going, and then this heart was locked.
But the dream was so great, as we wish it to never be done.
I fear now we must confess, *so false was our love…*

You Know It's Time

Towering walls of relentless snow and ash.
It moves on deeper now into my tired head.
The breaking manner of facts we still deny.
An unimpeded notion, yet we are still out of time...

Bitter judgment of the faces, pressing against the stone.
Now breathing alone in this shallow pool of blood.
Watching demons pull on the loose threads, *"hoping to come undone."*
But then God whispers a sigh and we all burn away, still out of time.

Crumbling concepts pushing harder alongside this heart.
Just a poor twisted bastard, waiting calmly within a shell.
Towering walls of frozen emotions, proving it was all but a lie.
As the angels pull the trigger, "you know it's time..."

Knife In the Desk

There must be a little demon living within my wrist.
As I begin digging it out, I wonder if it would ever be missed.
Just love-death, rage-pain, hate, hope and truth.
As I try and try, I just can't find the right words to explain this to you.

Still hoping upon a dream, now it's clear that I am insane.
As I break my teeth on the edge of this rusted blade.
More hysterical screams, rising from beneath my bed.
I laugh at you the one in the mirror, because I know you are dead.

There must be an answer, for that question we never asked.
Still I weep here scream-bleeding, with this knife in the desk.
For was it never the best, of all my scars felt so strange.
There must be a way out, so we burn all the remains...

Still hoping upon a dream, fears of when we were alive.
Please help me cut it out, the demon crawling up my spine.
Just give me not such a bitter motive, God free my pains!
Then as I pull the knife from the desk, I watch it bleed.
So it's just so fucking funny, that we truly are insane...!

Who Am I Today?

So who am I today? Just the demon on your shoulder.
What did God say? It blends with the distant thunder.
Where will we stay? When we admit this is over.
Who are you today? Maybe the Angel on my shoulder.

When *one* was once the traveling freak, there for but only the jest.
All so appropriate, as resting their heads upon the silk.
Down in the hallow, on is burning and felt deep in these lungs.
Not quite what they make of it, *yet soon to be at peace…*

So who am I today? Just another villain from the past.
What did she say? It's gone and won't come back.
Where did we land? When we both fell from above so high.
God who am I today? Maybe just a memory yet to fade…

This Knight Progresses

Upon a Golden sunset, our beautiful moon begins to sing.
Awake at present, as this knight progresses onward into the haze.
In expectation but then another of hells demons stands on the path.
So time once again to take blade in hand and stand firm.
Then the demon lunges forward, so very swift and composed.
A low slash then lifted high, separates the demon's scales upon its throat.
A burning liquid bleeds out, then seeps into the dirt across into nearby fields.
Burning a surrounding circle in which neither of us could escape.
"But I've made a promise to my love, a vow I shall never break.
To return home and to be at her side forever in love and grace…"
The demon dives forward, "so a fast counteract," then the demon leaps up.
Nine foot high the demon plunges from above, "No time to think!"
Blade shoved directly into the monster's heart, it lets out a sadistic gargled moan.
Then in one quick slash, off with the poor wretched things head.
The flames of hell bleed out of the demon's decapitated corpus.
Growing flames all around, "but I've made a promise I must never break!"
Then the moon exhales a cloud, and it brings on a cool summer rain.
Extinguishing all the flames of the burning felids and woods.
Now a clearer path is lain out before this knight's own two feet.
The moon smiles, embracing this knight calm upon his way.
But how many more demons lie waiting, to hinder all the road's lessons?
This knight fears not, "Just moving onward as this war progresses…"

U.F.O

Perhaps I am crazy, *"must have smoked something bad today."*
Eyelids begin to twitch, adrenaline pumping so I know I'm awake.
"Yes" I can see it, the metallic saucer hovering over an empty field.
I just can't fully illustrate it, the beautiful object in the sky.

So I venture a bit closer, towards the awesome metallic disk.
I look up at it, *still high enough to virtually see.*
It comes lower and then I begin to hear a light hum growing in my head.
I just don't know what it is in me, to make me smile and proceed.

Perhaps I am crazy, *"must have smoked something good today."*
I feel I can almost touch it, the alien craft that hangs above me.
It just seems so strange, that within I am now at peace.
As I watch myself being lifted off the ground, *"a bright flash of light."*
Then I awake alone in a field where there's no one else around.

Last One Standing

Just can't be there, as the hourglass spills out our past.
Where are we going now, God I do hope it to last.
Just a bit more intense, the tenderness of this broken mind.
But I believe I'm ready to be forgiven, I feel now that it is time…

For all that was once in the middle, between our words.
Lost now all that we have taken, and we never did learn.
As dark now like always and forever now so fucking dead.
These no longer feel like dreams, *so maybe you are erased from my head.*

So where are we all going, somewhere far beyond *the moons of Saturn*?
Who is it that flipped the switch, and brought forth the end of times..?
I can feel - only as all of my heart shatters, *now nothing left in my mind.*
Where is it that you all went to, somewhere so peaceful and fine?

For all that was once so lovely, held together in our hearts.
I just cannot be here, as the broken hourglass spills away our lives.
As so dark now here, I wonder where it is that everybody went.
So I guess I am the last one standing, *for now our world is fucking dead…*

Splitting the Pole

You go your way and I guess I'll go mine.
You say what you wish to say, that would be just fine.
You do that what you need to do, just speak up my friend.
You need only to be yourself, so go your own way again.

Splitting the pole, as our paths now have changed.
Soon to be cold, for nothing can stay the same.
We must be strong, as we fight for ourselves.
And we go our separate ways, deeper into hell...

As again now so overwhelmed, taking the next step.
We spilt the pole, as we go our own ways again.
It seems so strange, _that there is no time to explain..._
So we need only to be ourselves, as we go our separate ways.

"Eject!"

Climbing higher, the ground I can no longer see.
Into the heavens, where your selfish God never wanted me.
Reaching further, towards the stars and far beyond.
To the zenith, now at the end and all is done...

Climbing faster, the earth was but only a dream.
Reaching harder, now from my heart sorrow bleeds.
Must hold on a little longer, "can't seem to take this shit!"
Almost through the gates, then _all_ at once begins to slip.

Must "_Eject_," and just admit that I have failed.
Then falling faster, head first towards the flames of hell.
It's such a bother, the emotion of _a broken love_ and pride.
Free falling towards the ground, and I keep open my eyes.

Just like a demon, but I was once standing at the gates.
Forever I am hated, just one of our world's pitiful mistakes.
I have ejected, now falling deeper into the hells of my own fate.
A smile as I must admit, that I made this choice, to never be saved.

Smoking the Love-Note

She was an outward expression of my most inner self.
Presently now but a recollection, as I rummage through some old notes.
Being reminded of a time, a time when our love meant the world.
Now I feel only cold, so dark here as I rummage alone.

Digging through a pile of old notes, just rants and poetic nonsense.
Those pictures in my head, they're gone now – numb and faded sins.
From within-side I feel it scream, the tormented monster in my head.
Then I quote myself, *"you may have killed me my love but I'm not dead..."*

It all moves much faster, as the screaming voices won't ever cease.
Dark here in this room, surrounded by endless amounts of pages.
I feel I must admit, that today I am reasonably insane.
It feels like I'll never escape it, this damned distorted metaphoric cage.

But you know, I just cannot describe it.
The awesome fact that we have entered hell, forever now in the dark.
Demons upon endless demons, haunting my every thought.
I know I can never escape this, so I must admit that I am lost.

Just pages upon endless pages, in this sad sadistic tormented tome.
Then from between two sheets fell a single little love- note.
Notebook paper cut out into the shape of a heart.
It fell upon the desk, and then all in my head became so silent.

In the middle of the little cutout paper heart, she wrote, *"I love you."*
I held it so gently yet intent, for maybe just under an hour.
All in my mind so blank, cold dark and permanently awkward.
Then I burned the paper heart while still holding it in my hand.

A little heart of ash held so softly in the center of my burnt hand.
Still I can read the message she wrote to me, she said, *"I love you..."*
From within I can feel the demons scream, frantic in my head.
So I load the ashes into my pipe and then smoke it down into my lungs.

Holding my breath deep, and just waiting for the hatred to pass.
Just endless nonsense in my head, and a love-note burning in my chest.
It makes me believe that I'll never again be okay.
Then I exhale, and with the smoke all memories of her begin to fade...
"Always & Forever."

132

It Tasted Bitter

It tasted bitter, as you shoved the gun's barrel into my mouth.
All in my mind became but an undertone, so hushed and dulled out.
It did seem so strange to me, as my life flashed before my eyes.
It just tasted so bitter, then God spoke and said we would all be fine.

It felt so discomforting, as you pulled away the gun and dropped it to the floor.
Then I did say "you were boring, and nothing but a whore..."
But fact is fact, so go right ahead and push me once more.
Regardless if you pull the trigger, "you are still a whore..."

It tasted bitter, as then you spit your relentless venom into my brain.
Such a sweet drug, the one that burns so brutal but yet sooths all my aches.
So it is true I guess, that I am crazy, ready now to destroy this world.
It is just so bitter, "the damned fact that we will never learn..."

Voices Singing

Demonic voices singing inside my brain.
It sounds so soothing as it carries me away.
Within-side the discarded notions of *that past love*.
The voices continue singing on until the song is done.

Our lord God pushes his persistent chorus now onto me.
Through all of the horrific bloodshed and painful screams.
Need we now to see the inevitable burning of those remains?
The voices sing on endlessly, within my tormented headaches.

Shoved profoundly afar, then into the waking thought of our end.
Those voices sing their lyrics, so gallant and unyielding.
The Devil just laughs because he knows our story's secret twist.
My love - open your eyes before all of this beautiful insanity is missed.

For not then the reality of our disturbing conclusion.
The voices sing on and on so infinite within my heart and head.
Unfortunate that at one time I had said that "*I love you.*"
Suddenly the voices have stopped singing, because *we've reached the end.*

When I Held Her

As I held her, did I never think it would come to an end?
As in hell we burn, tormented perpetually over those senseless sins.
The clock now is broken, so I guess we're out of time.
Then more faded memories seem to surface, from the back of my mind.

As I held her, did I never think that it would last forever?
As I looked into her eyes, "just trying to keep my insane self together."
All of it meant so much in those days, now as only a thorn in my side.
The end was truly unavoidable, as is now the pain I can never again hide.

As I loved her, it seemed as if life had become but a beautiful dream.
Then sadly I awoke, awoke to the smell of my flesh as it is burning in hell.
It was the war that I battled, the *endless conflict* raging on within myself.
It was when I held her that I truly knew, *"we are dead now and nothing else."*

Sanity So Insane

Hold on tight, and let us now just fly away.
Into the silver and golden rainbows of so far beyond.
So take me there, and let us be not solitary in our shame.
Hold onto the needle, and then let us both now dissolve away.

Grip then onto the flesh, tear it back to reveal the truth.
What is it that waits hidden, under you're sick casing of lies.
"God take me there!" Into the middle of some better day.
Take my hand my love, let us fall now then again into our fears…

Embrace now the monster, for tomorrow shall shine release.
Taken then to the edge of the blade, now shoved deep within.
Into the darkness, *"GOD JUST GET ME OUT OF MYSELF!"*
It feels so brilliant, and then the smoke pulls it all away.

Hold on tight, and let us fly now to the so very far away.
Into the better thoughts, of maybe but sadly not today.
It feels so superb, so we need not to hide our shame.
"It's just so fucking funny, *this sanity so insane…"*

Halfway to Nowhere

So ready and unwilling, the heeding of what is yet to come.
Upon this thought for ages, as watching our reality coming undone.
Hard-pressed again to rise and battle, for this sad world of the weak.
It feels as if I can almost attain it, then I sink once more *below the waves*.

Halfway to *Nowhere*, but I do hope that I might arrive soon.
At the end of the rhyme now, here where our apocalypse blooms.
My hand now reaching, to gently wipe the tears from your eyes.
Now that the story is over, we need now only to smile and walk away…

So honored for the damage, within this soul lies our rotting hopes.
Away with the summer rains, all has become so fantastic and surreal.
Then into the searing flames that dwell within this monster's heart.
All that we believed in, *"sadly my love it was nothing more than a dream."*

As once when the demon spoke, persistent lustful voices into our heads.
Insanity has become so familiar, as I wait alone here under your bed.
Halfway to somewhere, hopefully soon I shall arrive to face the day.
Then again God tells me, this world is dead but it will be okay…

So ready for my chance now, to prove that I am more than a nonentity.
So rightfully deemed as the single soul that wanders this abyss.
Halfway to *Nowhere*, means I have only half a journey left.
To achieve that in which all this time I have been seeking.
As under the waves I take in a deep breath.
"Still halfway to Nowhere…"

Only Second Best

In the end it was funny I guess, that to you I was only second best.
I have tried yet failed, to justify that one lingering mistake.
I did love her to death once, but now unfortunately she is dead.
I wish to never again wake, so I close my eyes and hold my breath.

It's so sad to think, that to you I was only second best.
I did all I could in the matter, yet I fell short once again.
I did never mean for us, to end up this way at the end.
So now I must live with the fact, "that I was sadly only second best…"

Frequent Time-loss

Countless seconds and minutes bleeding from the clocks face.
Days upon weeks and months in which can never be replaced.
Years upon endless years which now are fading with the time-sands.
Here at the bottom of this hourglass, drowning in our _memories of then_.

As waking here at the dawn of these new poetic struggles.
Frequent as the needles seep deeper into my worthless brain.
So I stare back into the monster's eyes, concealing now all my pains.
But I fear that we can never out run it, soon we'll be only dust again.

As then into our inevitable loss of time and dying expectations.
The Devil speaks grim words of truth from the sleeping child's mouth.
So very frantic it is gushing, _seconds and minutes bleeding from the clocks face._
Days upon months and precious years which now can never be replaced.

Hog-Tied

How now to put those thoughts into words?
Was never felt as a tickle but a sick perverted hurt.
And again beyond those hopes of ever seeing the light.
Darkness has overwhelmed all in the _Angel's_ life.

Was meant to be a kind conversation over mutual associates.
It was nothing more than a lie off the wicked demon's breath.
The monster waited plotting all its demented perverse games.
But the little _Angel_ did not know, and was silently taken away…

The little _Angel_ awoke, hogtied alone somewhere in the dark.
As she woke she began to notice the sound of the demon breathing.
Her heart filled with fear as the little _Angel_ wept so cold and unaided.
Hogtied and screaming, as she watched the monster licking its teeth.

So how now to put this horrific story into words.
Of an _Angel_ that was convinced to step over the line and into hell.
It was all a lie of the monster, for so many years it had waited.
Now hogtied alone in hell, the _little Angel_ knows it can never escape it…

136

Broken Wing

"Never can seem to get a break."
Then once again all from my heart was sadly raped.
While screaming so madly at the top of my lungs.
But as nothing sounded, just had to watch myself come undone.

Here at the bottom of this twisted pit of false desires.
I want only to escape this but I just can not reach any higher.
So now I must admit, that as the lights went out, "I wasn't ready."
I was never ready, to live this nightmare against my will.

Just never can seem to get a break, as again my hopes were sadly raped.
Just need now to see it, the light that shines on the other side.
God I need to escape this, to maybe ease my troubled mind.
Sadly my wings are broken, so never again *"can I fly…"*

Activate

Throw the switch and let's watch all our atoms dissolve away.
When returned to the elements, that which makes us who we are today.
Are we ready, to achieve that honor of when we were alive?
Throw the switch and let us then kiss this fleeting reality goodbye.

Awake at the first touch of nonsense, drilling into my mind.
Are the voices speaking to me, from the riddle behind the rhyme?
When at the summit, God activates the *Armageddon* of our times.
So are we ready now, to watch as our world becomes but a dream…?

Activate now, the murder of that what lies beneath the rage.
Please just let me out, of this endless void that our Lord did make.
Help me to reach it, the switch that is waiting to be pressed.
Let us activate our own annihilation, as we let out our last breath.

Just throw the switch, the one that reads *"NO RETURN"*…
Then make a wish, *that maybe in the conclusion of this, that we might learn.*
God – as we release our breath, we are all now - so ready for rest.
"As we have senselessly activated the *Armageddon* of our times…"

Smoldering

Disorientating screams, cryptic hearts open and gushing.
Off the edge of the blade the rust bleeds, then into the weeping eyes.
We're left now at the answer, of the question that we wanted to ask.
Here in hell we are smoldering, and we can never again go back...!

Misplaced in dreams where none shall ever find me.
I am the awkward creature that sleeps beneath the flesh.
Of once then into our, _ill-gotten memories, leading into our beautiful deaths._
We are alone and forsaken, flames reaching miles above our heads.

Pulled aside at the dawn of that twisted remark.
For as of now, I am the cryptic message in which you seek.
Smoldering here beyond the horrific conclusion, known as only hell.
Lost for sure but never forgotten, that day when we both failed.

Distorted voices echoing, dancing so soothingly within my ears.
Here forever tormented in hell, taken over by all my fears.
God yes I am the silly creature, the demon that has seen the light.
Here in the deepest level of hell, where I've been waiting all my life...

Crippled & Waiting

Just can't focus, unable now to get a grip!
There at the bottom of the gutter, alone on my own trip.
Awaiting the reply, when the sky begins to fall from above.
But we cannot hide or out run it, we must pay for what we have done...

A twitch and I think there is something, moving within your brain.
So you dig hard to try and catch it, but it must have gotten away.
And in the distance you can hear the screams, so hollow and cold.
Oh it does seem that it's getting closer, then it scrapes against the bone.

Wide-eyed because there is definitely something wrong.
We can't seem to out run it, or hide in a place that is safe.
We can not move now, we are crippled and left here discarded.
Waiting and waiting for the stars to fall from the sky...

A Better Motive

Infinite allegories pumping throughout this poet's soul.
Tired illustrations alienated and never sold.
Now irritating this demonic yet once beautiful mind.
What new motives now, to drive all the pains away..?

It must be something, an omen of things yet to pass.
As the emotion of holding a love true, it *has now* relapsed.
For what this poet needs, an event to change the course time.
A better thought to hold, within this sick demented mind.

As a child - was known as the weak fragile little piece of shit.
As a man now - have been forgotten behind every riddle's twist.
Then in due time I might achieve, the answer given at the dawn.
Still it is that better motive I seek, within this poet's soul…

Infinite allegories swarming throughout this poet's brain.
Tired illustrations alienated and again it's all the same.
Now irritating this demonic yet once beautiful mind of peace.
It is that better motive I need, to drive away all the pain..?

My Ends

So duly noted, that which we must never speak.
The gun is loaded, so let us now begin the parade.
A spectacle that you would never expect to see.
As we dance our own deaths into the grave.

But I believe there is an injustice, now left astray.
With time the scars have been hidden, yet still she feels the shame.
The gun is loaded as the clock-hands keep spinning around.
Had in the past been naïve, and now below the waves she drowns.

So duly noted, that which has lost all its allure.
The gun is loaded, so the trigger is pulled and the tears hit the floor.
Like thousands of raindrops, seeping deep into the flesh.
So did my ends truly justify the means or was it all a waste of breath?
"So cold now as she drifts away…"

Charred Remains

In years passed, did the moon ever seem so close?
As if you could just reach out and take it for yourself.
I do love this emotion that I feel, so warm and comforted.
But the moon is vanishing and I think I'm out of time.

IN GOD'S GOOD NAME, _"WHAT THE FUCK IS THIS!?"_
A dried blood stain on the floor in the middle of the back room…
OH NO - I THINK I'M GONNA FREAK OUT, _"YES I KNOW I AM!"_
I do remember that day when she stayed awake all night weeping…
I JUST CAN'T SEEM TO TAKE THIS SHIT, _"OH PLEASE GET ME OUT!"_

In years passed, was ever there a time when you had smiled.
As if you were in a dream-world where no one has ever felt pain.
I do truly love this emotion I feel, so detached and at ease.
But then again I sadly merge with reality and awake again in pain.

SO WHAT NOW HOLDS ENOUGH REASON, _"OTHER THAN SIN!"_
She was always awkward in that beautiful way that I grew to love…
THEN ALL AT ONCE MY WORLD WAS RAPED, _"LEFT BLEEDING!"_
But when I held her I began to know that all of our love was taken away…
GOD PLEASE SAVE US, _"FROM THE FACT THAT WE ARE DEAD!"_

It was years passed, when sobriety illustrated the truth.
That battle after relentless battle, in the war still remains the same.
I do love this, the fact that in the end no one will win.
Only charred remains will be left, as now we burn for all our sins.

Chapter 8

The Hand That Feeds You.

First Person

Such a feeble mind, dwelling within darkness day after day.
A picture of an angel painted on the wall, in red blood it is stained.
All at once the zombies laugh, so demonically moving.
It is this void of darkness, known as the dreamer's mind…

Was I the first person, to recognize the corruption of my young soul?
At the end of the shadow, torn edges and *a message* to endure.
For at the dawn now of this new metaphorical paradigm.
I believe that I was the first person, to dissect my own troubled mind…

As led to accept, "at the end of this story I will surely be dead."
In this fucked up first-person perspective, I see now that this is it.
The twisted truth that our great tome did never foresee.
And that secret shall remain hidden, deep in the sleeper's dreams...

For You to Hate

Tongue-less screaming, I must manage all my waking fears.
Wingless flying, to the other side of that bitter morning.
Now look inside, and then tear in deep!
This shattered heart is broken, so let us just sleep.
But we are never to find a point, there is sadly no greater reason.
I am mad, truly now I know that I am dead?!

Living this life, as finding new monsters under my bed.
Little winged demons digging their way deep into my head.
Here so twisted I sway, forever now so fucking insane!
Loss of mind, and I know that I am meant for you to hate.
Never finding any reason, truly only my waking fears.
Then the sky rains boiling LSD, seeping into all my thoughts.
Must I die and fade away?
I know I only exist, for you to hate…

The River Dry

Pride so betrayed and broken, for now the river runs dry...
We look to the heavens but no salvation seems to shine.
Her love has driven me over the edge, "I laughed as I fell."
All I have ever felt was pain, and lust still rings true.
"Too far gone – I have lived so long? Long away from sane."
Still sorrow remains for now all the rivers run dry...

Just logic of the truth, it eats at me from deep inside.
All I have ever wanted, it doesn't seem the same without her.
Please give me hope, that someday we might reach the next page...
Night blooms within my heart, and I never was really sane.
It was that lust, the sin that brought us to this funny twist.
So I cut in deep trying to find an end, and I do know.
As all the rivers run dry, I laugh falling so cold.

Vacant Chest

Was darker then, as the snow began to flood this mind.
I am nothing but a dying whim, just far too gone to be alright.
This vacant chest, empty now for so many long years.
It was so much darker then, all those times that I thought you cared...
A smile as insanity begins, here in this odd world that I did make for me.
When again those thoughts of our laughter continue, "Get me out of my sanity!"
Led then into the past, this mind caving in on itself.
So tormented again, agony and the hammering pain of needles is all that is felt.
Once more the voices scream, unending is the memory that roams in my brain.
Haunted for so very long, and to think that they all said it would be okay...
Now on a better roll, and this hidden murder remains lost.
Somewhere near a lake, all the snow flooding her tomb.
It was darker then, now this chest is vacant as is my tired head.
For now left only to bleed, into the center of that waking lie.
Hollow may be the correct word to use, for it is now that time.
To follow through with the campaign, marching onward into death.
Numb and I feel not a thing, as so vacant is my chest.

144

As We Forget Her Name

Slow this down then catch the wrist.
Ten million more miles until all is missed.
For as anger is steaming, just want my apathy all for me.
Now slow it down and let the tide come as we both dream.

No – just can't fight it now, the grim truth of shame.
As beneath the abyss it drowns, nothing now is the same.
So show us please what it is that brings the pain to an end.
For we are not the same now, nor shall we ever be again...

As we forget her name, what is it that brings on the hate?
As she was my greatest mistake, I still would never change.
But all is lost now, just a memory that is sadly dying.
So we forget her name, as it's washed away in the fire.

Beautiful whipping flames, so gentle all our hopes die.
As we forget her name, that chapter is erased from this mind.
Just slow it down and then maybe we can see a better side.
For now her name is forgotten, yet sadly so is mine...

Fragments of the Past

Hello out there, my friend on the other side of the page.
Please read on, so we can find out which one of us is insane.
As the edge is broken off, blood gushing down onto the floor.
This is but a fragment of the past, a reality that is no more.

The ministry has come and now carnage is all that remains.
Of then into the truthful lies that prove this is what was meant to be.
Scattered all throughout, endless fragments of the past.
Please tell me my friend, when will all of this pain come to an end?

Hello out there, to you my love who is reading this today.
Can together we gather all the fragments of the past that are left astray.
Please get me there, to that comfortable place in your heart.
Please just read on, to prove that we were truly never insane...

Reverting Darkness

We were once the truth, of the so faded away and lost.
For now we decay and then slip away, into the sound-sorrow of our madness-joy.
Can't stand to be the monster they hate but there is nothing to say.
O yes, the time has come, so let us prepare now to be judged.
Then again you crumble away, as here in the hourglass I sleep and sway.

Marching on further, deeper into the darkness of hell.
Such a poetic talent, the dreaming child so overwhelmed.
There are new ways to describe it, the wound in the middle of this chest.
Can't stand to think it, that this endless nonsense is all that's left.

We were once the hope, of this failing dream known as humanity.
For now we have become, the nonentity that shall never be saved.
Just can't stand this, to be the unknown answer that our world seeks.
Then again all begins to crumble, reverting to darkness as we all sleep...

Our Separate Ways

I suppose, that we are now but only at the end.
I could scream at the top of my lungs for days, *"just the same as then."*
We held on for hours, yet only to watch the tide recede.
So now we go our separate ways, so time now to breathe.
For we both seek an answer, which is unable to be found.
We held on so long, and just could never let go.
Today we must admit that hell has become cold.
We are breaking down again, only salt will remain.
Our brains begin to twist and we know that we are insane.
Then set aside all that mattered and again we both fall away.
Nothing at the bottom of this pit, still just falling away.
As screaming louder, we must now go our separate ways.
I suppose now, that this is but only the end.
We must admit that the story is over, and we start a new page.
We held on for hours, just trying to gain some sort of new hope.
We have gone our separate ways, and now hell is so cold...

Judging the Wicked

For honor of a noble gambit, then thrust into horrific queries.
We are judging the wicked, those who oppose the appropriate jest.
"It feels like rust and broken glass rising up, then regurgitated on the floor."
For what the little creatures speak, from the other side of the mirror.

So can we discuss pride toady to set an opinion that might stand?
Yet still the clouds rain, flooding this feeble world once again…
So smile like you mean it, as we violently tear off God's face.
We're judging the wicked, and yet we are the same.

True honor lost, as our unavoidable overture has failed.
So I guess we broke the ice and now the *Devil* weeps alone in his mind.
"It seems as if all has ended, we are all now but a memory yet to pass."
Still we are judging the wicked, those who oppose the appropriate jest.

So can we argue pride today or is this not the right time?
And still the clouds rain, flooding this twisted poetic mind.
So smile like you mean it, as we so viciously tear off our God's face.
As still we are judging the wicked, and yet we are the very same…

If I Never Tried

As once upon a twisted down-lift.
Had no choice but to cut open my eye.
To bleed out all that I had once seen.
And still you had the nerve, to say I never tried.

If I never felt, that one time you said it was love.
Realizing that this is hell, and from the sky rains ash and blood.
If I never lied, then why now is my heart so cold?
Here in this broken cage, knowing I truly have no soul.

As once upon a fucked up down-lift.
Had no choice but to admit, that my thoughts are truly unique.
Then again to bleed out, all that I had ever seen.
If I never tried, then it really must be true.
That I am insane, and so are you…

The Right Fuse

It is now time, to dig into my rotten brain.
Just smile again my love, as you rip the flesh off of my face.
Then acid pours down, as I swing above the stairs.
The right fuse must be gone, and now we're out of air.

Time has become a pointless bitch, but it's running out.
And with your teeth, you pull out the stitch.
Now gallons of blood just gushing down.
For now there is a newer reason, but I must not tell.
LSD upon my lips, and beyond the mirror we both see hell.

It is now time, for you to dig into my rotten brain.
Endless gallons of blood, and a notion never replaced.
Was it the right fuse, the one that broke in my head?
It is now time to find an answer, but you turned off the lights instead.

Waiting In Myself

So dark out here, this dead space that has no name.
Pissed away another year, so again it's all the same.
I think that I had died today, or maybe just opened my eyes.
So dark as I wait in myself, this endless poetic mind.

So cold out here, this void within my brain.
I ripped out all of my teeth, and smashed my forehead against the grave.
I've had enough of the nonsense, no more time for games.
I'm so sorry that I loved you, but that was my mistake.

So dead out here, just waiting alone in myself.
She once had a name, but it was erased when we chose hell.
There is no better sacrifice, only time is now lost.
But I did once say I loved you, no matter what the cost.

So dark in here, broken weeping as waiting in myself.
I did have the chance to save us, but instead I chose hell.
I've once tried to stop you, from running so far away.
But I am glad that you're gone now, I have no time for these games.

"Ojo"

Truly I can never seem to find a better reason for me to breathe.
This world is beating me down, and I fear now that I am unseen.
The lights are fading, only the echoes of screams remain in this heart.
And *Truth* drips off the edge of the blade, as again I am torn apart.

Then death drops *from off the razor*, as your twisted love holds me true.
Life was so short, and I wish I could have spent more time with you.
I see now the only truth, is that all I ever really needed was you.
To save me from this unending torment.
Still your eyes stare up at me, reminding me that I am truly insane.

Because we were once friends, together until the end of time.
But forever was never long enough, now so empty in this mind.
Only snow and ash remain, up to my eyes in the torment.
But you must understand and feel, that - what you see in me.
Thousands of hands pressing against me, all over my shattered surface.
Yet sadly *"the world,"* will never truly see…

Weed

Drop me deep then into the past, dope me sweet and hope it to last.
See me in the back room, writhing alone in sorrow and rage.
Soon now we'll both be nothing but gone and wasted.
Love felt with every breath, so forever and always wasted.

Just trying to keep these thoughts straight, as they wander around.
Then I begin to feel the bones break, and you scream so loud.
For there is now no mistake, only the truth that they hide.
Then another breath taken, and I believe that we will be fine.

Just drop me deep beyond the past, dope me now and hope it lasts.
See me there, laughing below the growing cloud of smoke.
As the weed keeps on burning, I know that I'm not alone.
So dope me true and let me say that I did this all for you...

And again I seem to have lost my train of thought, felt so wasted.
So dope me now to set us free, but it's all okay.
"So dope us sweet."

The Zombie Takes Control

Locked so tight but then I seem to break these eyes open.
From beneath the dirt so cool, but un-soothing.
These hands reach up above the surface moving aside the lumps of grass.
This body now awake again, and yet all else seems to be dead.

There is no one here, this dead empire of memories and ghosts.
This zombie stands tall, but for what now is the greater reason.
The moon it whispers, that silent melody into this decaying heart.
I am the king now, the only remaining corpse.

So dark here as the black sun rises, once again upon this dawn.
I have searched this world for so many ages, to find I am alone.
So frozen within this mind, I guess I was never truly alive.
But now I stand in control, of this rotten dead empire.

For once upon a time, I might have been the angel on your shoulder.
But it is true that I am dead and just waiting to fade.
I did once save you, yet still you lie alone in your grave.
And that I cannot deny, as I wander awake and so cold.

Locked so tight, this heart now broken open.
Tar and blood gush out, so I know I'm full of nonsense.
I just can't save us, for I see now that our world is truly dead.
I am the zombie that has taken control, to save this world in your head.

Only Sorrow

It was a shock to me, as I watched the blade remove the flesh.
It was so funny to me, below the waves - so out of breath.
Only sorrow remains, that is all I have at this time.
So come then and follow me, to the other side of the line.

It was a shock to me, as you pushed me over the edge.
It was funny to me, that I fell for years and never hit.
It is endless now, and sadly only sorrow remains.
So come then now and follow me my love.
To the other side of this page.

150

LandMine

Alpha team is dead, we lost contact at dawn.
The enemy is upon us now, I fear we won't last long.
We march on for hours knowing what lies ahead.
We must escape this war, locked in our own heads.

Extraction point is far now, so we must push ahead swiftly.
Move on now quicker, heads down and silent!
Must have been only a bird, no-no we are being watched.
Sniper bullet through a comrade's head, and now all hope is lost.

We are here now, at this battle field we must make a stand.
Fight on now and die with honor, until no man stands.
We have made it my brothers, we are almost out.
I've stepped now onto a land mine, so I smile as I let my breath out.

"Live on my soldiers, live to fight another day..."

Stone Fields

Thousands upon thousands towering into the sky.
The text is now faded but the story has not died.
I am searching for that one, it must be here.
These endless stone fields, evoking only fear.

With blood spilt down, the small amount upon the coin.
The dust bleeds out, our souls null and void.
Our flesh melts off, proving we are the same.
Searching these stone fields, for that once forgotten name.

Yes thousands upon thousands towering into the sky.
For at this point I must question that fact I wish to deny.
But it must be true, all though I might never find.
Within these endless stone fields, our story that has died.

The Day We Touched

Gazing deep as the truth flows out of her soft blue eyes.
All has stopped for but only a moment in time, "smiles as I bleed."
To watch as the walls turn, or maybe it's only me.
For time wasting, my world shattered and pasted to the floor.
Still I think I can remember, what lies beyond that open door.

So damn hazy, can't make out my own hand in front of my face.
I hope that this might all make sense, maybe one of these days.
As gazing deep, into her beautiful soft blue eyes.
I can recall the day, the day when we first touched and felt alive.
So awkward yes, but still it remains somehow frozen in time.

All has stopped now but for only a brief moment.
Still I wish that I can save us, but today I just cannot reach.
As gazing deep and watching as the truth flows out from her soft blue eyes.
So damn cold out here, in the middle of my pain filled mind.
I can no longer recall the day we touched, but I guess we'll both be fine.

Out Of My Mind

I feel I'm falling, so far out of my mind.
The passion was calling, then I fell upon the other side.
Into our once forgotten, twisted thoughts of faith.
Now so far out of my mind, I shall never be the same.

At this point now, I realize my heart is but a stone.
At this point now, here in Hell all alone.
Truly out of my mind, and in the mirror lies a faceless mistake.
At this point now, the Devil and God knows it is too late.

I feel I'm falling, so very much unseen.
Into the abyss I am calling, here below the sea.
At this point now, we are forgotten, lost somewhere in space.
We are truly out of my mind, so it really is all the same.

So Far From Grace

Here I stand now so far from grace.
With this rusted blade, I now cut off my face.
To hand to you, my love beneath the dirt.
I am so far from grace, and I know I'll never learn.

Here I scream now, so very far from grace.
And she whispered, that silver bullet through my brain.
So I weep now, rotting beneath a tree.
Gone now and forgotten, the memory that should never be.

There you stand now, so very far from grace.
Then we cut down, and peel off each other's face.
So you speak now, your predictable poison below the flesh.
So far from grace now, screaming without a breath.

Show the Way

Dig in deep, below the flesh, so you can see the way.
Open eyes and so very blind, the purple demon with her face.
Laugh now and scream, tearing to the bottom of what you seek.
Dead bodies all around, and I know that they are me.

Brought then beyond the torment, of what hides inside.
The government tries to deny it, but we know it's a fucking lie.
We weep now all together, flooding this pathetic world.
So I reach out, to save you, but then I watched you burn.

Dig in deep, beyond the flesh, come on Satan and show the way.
Mercy is dead, so off with your head, and bleed quiet in shame.
So forgotten naught, the angel so lost and she will never find her way.
So taken last, deep into the past, where pride remains contained.

Show the way, beyond the gates, where all the angels sing.
Throw me down, below the clouds, into Hell where I should be.
Dig in deep, then open eyes, and you know who I am.
Show the way, beyond the shame, where angels and demons weep.

They Call It Fear

There it is breathing right behind you, and you can feel it on the back of your neck.
It is laughing as it's waiting, just picking its moment to attack.
They call it fear, the emotion running cold down your spine.
They call it fear, the fact that you are out of time.

In the darkness you begin to see the monster's grin.
You cannot outrun it, your back is now against a wall.
No time to think, there is no prayer now to save this soul.
They call it fear, as it runs up your spine so cold.

What the fuck now to say, with screams echoing against the walls.
Darkness consuming within my veins, as fear takes my fragile soul.
What am I to do then, I just watched you walk away.
I cannot say I'm sorry, because you never existed anyway.

There it waits creeping, the phantom behind the stage.
They call it fear, that which waits in the darkness of our mistakes.
You cannot deny me, for I am that translucent ghost.
They call it fear, that which controls our fragile souls.

This Angel's Wings

Resurrected, the notion of being a shallow fuck.
All lost forever, and I should've looked away.
Cannot be myself now, so I step over and down.
Behind the open door, and upon the golden clouds.

"For I am the Demon with Angel-Wings, not said the same and still it sings."
Then betrayed for reasons, truly unknown to me.
Resurrected, beyond the notion of being a poetic mistake.
Upon God's twisted nature, I was then cast away.

This angel's wings upon the demon known as I.
All lost forever, and I'll never know why.
Neglected for ages, lost behind a forgotten page.
I am the nonentity that you once cast away.

The Sandman Comes

Kicking frantic as the sheets are being pulled from the foot of my bed.
I am screaming, but mommy doesn't really give a damn.
Somebody please save me, I know he wants to have his way.
Mommy save me, but then the sandman comes, and takes me away.

An odd world it is, the land known as my dreams.
The sandman has taken me to a place I do not want to be.
The monsters are clawing, reaching and snarling, they want to feed.
An odd world this truly is, my nightmare known as me.

Kicking so frantic as falling miles and miles and miles and miles more.
The sandman comes again, and takes me within his demonic world.
A dream they call it, but no desires here are met.
Only torment as the sandman takes me deeper into my own head.

I am screaming, weeping, please somebody save me.
Get me out of here, but the door is locked, I cannot escape.
This is my real living nightmare, the fact that I am insane.
The sandman comes, it is getting dark now and soon I will be away.
Please Mommy save me, un-blanket me so I can awake.

My Naïve Heart

As spoken upon those soft words bleeding into the stone.
A hard lesson but it is a truth that we must know.
Truly unavoidable, the tragic inevitable fact.
Still I wish to deny it, and then I know she'll never come back.

Heart beating, stapled out of order and lost.
Truly never to die, for I am that which will always be.
As then spoken soft upon those words that bleed within the stone.
Such a hard lesson to learn, but you know it in your soul.

So lock us in, deep into the waking notion of our dismay.
Razor separating all the notions so you believe that it is the same.
My heart still wishes to deny it, the inevitable fact which I hate.
Still I know it is true, the grim reality that I am erased...

Sophisticated Perspectives

You push it, you push it, you want your opinions to stand.
Am I but your scapegoat dancing now upon another rant?
It is curious indeed, how you judge and condemn.
You wish to be jury, execute all which oppose.

Deeply now conspiring against this thought that remains just.
You push your sophisticated perspectives and wish us not to oppose.
We should just stand here, and smile as the atom bomb falls.
I am but only your scapegoat, the individual you wish lost.

So how does it feel up there, as upon that pedestal you stand?
Perched so high with an eagle's eye, ready now to strike.
Truly it is pointless, to push your ideals onto me.
I need not to see through your eyes, *for you are blind and forever will be.*

You push it, you push it, your knife deep into my back.
I am now bleeding dry, I can't believe this has happened again.
Through all your sophisticated perspectives, did you predict this end?
As now all is gone, beyond your sophisticated perspectives of sin.

I've Failed God...

I failed God, when I stepped over the ledge.
I let go and let out my breath with a laugh.
I was a dreamer who did never find sleep.
I was the sleeper whom never did dream.

I failed God, when I swallowed down the razor.
I let it all go, and then admitted that there was no one greater.
I am high now, numb straight to my core.
I am hungry, lost in a desert *that is not of this earth.*

I failed God, when I had said "*Always & Forever.*"
I had to let go and just admit that all was truly over.
For I am the dreamer whom did never *wake.*
I've failed God, as once again now I see that I am awake.

Raining Maggots

Such a sour smell in the air, the clouds so dull.
Thunder cracking through the sky and now growing cold.
The wind it picks up, a storm coming today.
I believe now it is raining, but something seems very strange.

A rain drop has fallen, and landed on my face.
I can feel it writhing, so I pull it away.
It's a fucking maggot, that has fallen from the sky.
Then it comes a downpour, raining maggots all through the night.

Such a sour smell in the air, rotten meat and maggots flooding this land.
There is something really fucking wrong with this picture.
It seems as if the gates of Hell have opened in the sky.
All the maggots have now morphed, into demonic butterflies.

Swarms upon endless swarms, blackening out the sun.
They tear the flesh off all that they come upon.
So I try to find shelter, a cellar below my broken room.
But it is locked, so I guess I'm fucked and so are you.

Duality

I feel great now, now that the man in the mirror is dead.
But he is awake now, oh no not again.
So I'm a freak now, I guess you always knew I would be.
The true end to this fucked up world that we chose for you and me.

We are at the end now and still you are biting the hand that feeds you.
It makes no sense now, because it has still yet to begin.
I wish that you would understand once what it means to be alive.
We are both the same again, but will never truly be.

I feel so fucked now, I am truly out of my own head.
But I think I'm home now, but I know it never did exist.
So I am the freak then, the man that you grew to hate.
We are the same now, and yet we'll never be again.

Chapter 9

My Cynical Friend

Breaking My Neck

Ready to accomplish now, something in which I've never done did.
Here breaking my neck, as looking back over all our sins.
We are ready true, to hold the light between me and you.
Here at the end of *our world*, we know we are free...

Ready now to take that step, beyond the line and into the ash.
Breaking my heart over the truth, hidden deep in the past.
Are you ready, to take that step a million miles down?
Then we breathe in, and yet we never drown.

Here now breaking, all of what has made me, *Me...*
True is the grim fact, which lingers in my sleep.
I am smiling, at the weeping face in the mirror.
I have broken its neck, so now we can see hell much clearer.

I'll Race You

Ready. Set. Go.
I'll race you to that place, behind the open door.
I'll take you to a place, left dark and broken on the floor.
So shallow it screams, the demented child wishing for hope.
I'll race you now, beyond the cloud, "*And then we stare into Satan's eyes.*"

It stands there bold, the statue reaching beyond the sky.
It is the face of God, now our world hopes to deny.
The power of the *Atoms*, breaking away all we hold.
I'll race you, to the other - side of this story untold.

Ready. Set. Go.
I'll race you as we fall down the rabbit's hole.
Into a better trip, beyond sorrow and dismay.
And I feel I'm gonna be sick, and I know now we are insane.
I'll race you, far beyond the words of the beast.
I'll race you, to the end of this twisted infectious disease.
I'll race you, now ready - set - Go!

Equal Exchange

Something once given then equally received.
Upon more twisted notes dancing behind the screens.
It is for that notion taken, now more of a better breath.
Was once something taken, given back then at first chance.

Tomorrow's lies can't change it, we are erased away.
A life for a death, a death for a life, that is equal exchange.
Left whispering little voices, that sing within my ear.
Reminding me of my death, and erasing next year.

Something once given, then equally received.
Upon no more of a divine nature, lingering behind the screens.
It is this notion, taken once and never given back.
Was once something equal, exchanged and never again has a chance.

Liberty & Justice

Logic left weeping, heavy tears of pride.
Within these veins, pumping black ash and bloody slime.
Was once a noble action, now just another pointless rhyme.
Thrust deeper beyond the shadows, known as our minds.

He stands there weeping, concrete words bleeding from his thoughts.
His brother has died, so for now hope is lost.
A solider has sacrificed, his life so we can live free.
His brother stands weeping alone, but honored that he is still free.

Logic left screaming, rusted nails into the spine.
Within this heart, pumping backwards and now dead inside.
Was true that it doesn't matter, and there is sadly now no return.
Liberty and justice left weeping, on this night so very cold....

162

Show Some Mercy

Show some mercy before you push us over the line.
Show some mercy right before we turn off the light.
Scream just nonsense, it is what makes you unique.
Scream just nonsense, a bitter end known as me.

Show the better path now, then wake me at the dawn.
Show a better path now, for we have held on too long.
We are at the end now, trying to say that it made sense.
We are at the end now, and it is just the same as then.

Take my heart out, then rape it before God's eyes.
Take my heart out, and drink from it the rusty lime.
Say you care now, and yes that would be so sweet.
Say you care now, behind those twisted words of deceit.

Bleed for a better reason, and we are running out of faith.
Bleed for a better reason, and admit that we are disgraced.
Show some mercy, before you pull the trigger and laugh.
Please show some mercy, before you turn your head *and never look back.*

In-Sane

Got to admit now that we are insane.
Dancing with Devils upon her grave.
Just screaming with angels.
As wishing to fall.
I am now in Hell.
And it doesn't matter at all.

Got to awake now for I am insane.
The mirror is broken as shattered is my face.
I am just wishing to weep now.
Alone, broken, and so cold.
Here upon the truth now.
Parading with my fears.

Surgery With a Spoon

Do you want to hear some fucked up shit?
At one point it might make you sick.
A story of pain, torn flesh, and blood.
Of when I performed surgery, with a fucked up rusted spoon.

Was a long road that year, thousands of miles left behind.
Had just to escape it, all the demons that were eating at me.
Many miles walked upon the roads that lead to anywhere.
Then lost again, heart filled with sin, and I never did learn.

Feet worn down, bones scraping against the road.
Heat beating down, this road taking my soul.
Then I felt a stab, at the bottom of my feet.
Thousands of blades of grass, forever stabbing into me.

Then I begin to notice, that I'm dragging a fucking nail.
Have no choice but to remove it, with whatever I can grasp.
Only a fucking rusted spoon, and I guess it will have to do.
Time to dig it out, God damn this surgery that must ensue.

It doesn't come out easily, it does take a few minutes.
The bottoms of my feet caked in tar and rotten blood.
But then I removed it, the nail at the bottom of my feet.
It was straight to the bone, but that is nothing new I say.
It truly was irrelevant, so I just threw it away.

Family Feast

It wasn't me, it wasn't me.
Waiting behind that open door.
It was the end, the demon of sin.
Waiting within, this shattered mind.

It was a feast, it was a feast.
Tasting so deliciously sweet.
It was to be, so generally twisted at the end.
But they are all gone now.
And your family shall never return again.
They're all gone…

It Wasn't Me

It couldn't be, no I couldn't see.
For the lights were blinding my tired eyes.
Below the sea, echoing vibrant screams.
I looked into my eyes, and it wasn't me.

For death to taste, now such a waste.
I am a goddamn nonsense, weeping and bleeding on the floor.
For hours too late, cannot clean off the slate.
I've spoken with myself, and it wasn't me.

Now dare to dare, then flesh it tears.
How do you feel as you wear my face?
For not ever again to breathe, here in these hollow dreams.
I have awakened to see, it wasn't me.

On the Kitchen Floor

Held in my arms for never-more, so cold can barely breathe.
For I am the nonentity within your soul, dig in and try to see.
You are the nonsense that I hold, so very hidden in the past.
How much longer can I remain, to keep the truth from coming back?

Push once more your fingernails, below the flesh and into the spine.
Taste the insanity that is gushing forth, bleeding out into your hands.
Was once a story untold, and I dared not to think it to resurface again.
Of a demonic act, lying there shattered on the kitchen floor.

God I know it wasn't me, but the truth haunts still indeed.
This pressure is building, and I can't seem to take this shit.
All points have been loaded, so go ahead and make a wish.
Again we know it is pointless, to kill that which has never lived.

Now once more into the nightmare, far beyond the road of leaves.
Into a pit of boiling tar, hell is where sanity has kept me.
There was once a story, of a horrific death on the kitchen floor.
But again I must hide the truth, far behind the open door.

Inside - Untold

Wake up now and see, as fire is raining from the sky.
Disorganized indeed, bitter truths and sweet little lies.
Rip back the question, of what makes you who you are.
I truly am the answer, waiting within the shallow scars.

Hold on and wish it, to simply just fade away.
Fear because we want to, of the monster below my grave.
Weep out tears of distrust, the fact is we are alone.
Slap me now because I am a pointless fuck, *whom never did make any sense.*

So what is it you hide inside – untold.
The truth of a fact that you have denied for years.
That we have murdered, hope has died behind our tears.
Now truly I can see, this is now the end to be.

Just a Nothing

Too many times and so many lies.
My trust was given through, and then I fell for you.
So like it or not, all emotions now rot.
With my hands around your neck, it is your pain I love best.

Then spilt onto the concrete, honor and pride of death.
Was once a great world of justice, now no one gives a shit.
I am the little Satanist, whom did follow the path of the lord.
I am a fucking heretic, annoyed with you because you are absurd.

Now passion is so distant, and fucking torn away.
My shame cannot contain it, I fear we are insane.
I am just a fucking nothing, whom never did belong in this world.
I am what it is you fear, waiting for you behind the mirror.

*Upside-Down Penn*y

Headed now away from this place, this fucked up hollow shell.
Still miles away until we can say, that it all made a little sense.
The candles burn and you'd think we'd learn, *still we provoke the beast.*
I can't see it now, I can see it now, the demon that holds my name.

There is no face, there is no taste, light, emotion, or hope at all.
There is only the thought, of now all is lost, so we need just to breathe.
So take me there, never take me there, it is eternal hell.
But the medicine helps, I'm calm now, so I guess I'm okay.

No chance ever again to hold it, it is frittered away into the past.
Cut then small layers off of the surface of my eyes.
Paste them on, to see the inevitable truth you still wish to deny.
God fuck it now, there is no hope, it is an upside-down penny.

Drama

There it goes now, hammering against my skull.
Pathetic little voices, begging for control.
They wish to push their drama into the foreground for all to see.
But the more they try and push it, it keeps eating at me.

Can't stand all the bullshit, that they tried to say is real.
We must now admit, that some wounds cannot be healed.
There is at this moment, no time to understand one truth.
But like it or not, it has nothing to do with you.

There it goes again, all their persistent nonsense against my skull.
I am ready now to dig deeper, until I reach the bone.
Justice in this fucked up nonsense, you try to make it stand as your point.
Fuck you and all your drama, your Goddamn unending pathetic noise.

Etched In My Skull

I can feel it now, so brutally etched into my skull.
The needle is out, numb and I feel all is locked.
Lights are spinning, so very fast around my head.
The answers are all lost, or maybe it is me again.

Can't stand to be there, watching you grow disgraced.
As you laughed and grinned, of yes I knew it was the same.
Betrayal was constant, as is this torment inside.
I could feel now, my mind screaming, echoes so deep behind.

The demon speaks cold and quiet, waiting behind the stage.
Broken glass does surround it, no we cannot escape.
Take now and just begin to forget it, it was just a pointless whim.
It was etched in my skull for a meaning, unknown now even to me.

Distorted Life

Take us far, beyond this bitter distorted life.
A little maggot, at the bottom of the jar begins to wish for flight.
It writhes and wriggles, hoping to escape its cage.
Then it begins to transform, into a demon with a human's face.

Take us very far, beyond this hollow, twisted, distorted life.
Take one step back, to see behind the page.
Not all has come to end yet, yes still we believe that we were sane.
Marching on further, parading about in this bitter distorted light.

Take us much deeper, into the core of what was once my heart.
Just admit that death has spoken, and it has torn us all apart.
You are a better nonsense, truly my cynical friend.
Into this distorted life, I lead the path now once again.

Mushroom Breath

The music notes begin to bend.
Creating a twisted tornado inside my mind.
I can taste it now, so sweet it burns upon my tongue.
The sour poison in which you once wept.
From your beautiful soft blue eyes.
The pressure screams then once again.
As Satan rolls his tongue upon the back of my eyes.
I wanted to cease, this conflict in me.
The proud truth, that we did not survive.

Deadened Heartbeats

Eternal echoes they roll.
Faded notions left upon the stone.
Then why left between two brothers.
A knife in the back and a slap in the face.
We did try once to save each other.
Yet we hold now only, these deadened heartbeats.

The Heavenly Father

All praise now the Heavenly Father.
All give rejoice and hopes to be saved.
All admit now that we are sinners.
All is done now and we are in our graves.

Push then back the only chance of we know how.
Cut deep into the center, and only tar is pulled out.
Weep now Mother, you cannot save me tonight.
Forgive me please my Father, but I fear now it is time.

All praise now the Heavenly Father.
All place your hands together, in prayers to be saved.
All admit that we are demons.
All is dead now, and in the grave.

Nine Years Ago

Looking back now, I can see that it was surreal.
As the small creature rushed along the fence.
Heading far into the back, into the tall grass.
Still I don't know why I chased after the odd little creature.

Must've been curious to see the alien beast.
Intrigued in what it is that hides in the dark.
But never did I find an answer to that night.
Still I begin to question, whether I was wrong or right.

Looking back now, I did smoke a lot of fucking weed.
Must've been something great for me to trip so very far.
It was nine years ago, and still I am haunted by the little creature's face.
Looking back now, I have to admit that shit was insane.

Reality Or the Dream?

Very many times I have been confronted.
Whether to live a reality or a dream.
A smile given, then poetic thoughts begin to bleed.
She was the motive, yet now a memory that is haunting me.

Soft steps upon the leaves, leading into the dawn.
Blood it tastes so sweet, as it drips from off her tongue.
Mother Earth, she is screaming, for we have now gone blind.
That is the sad reality from which I cannot attempt to doubt.

She was very soothing, calming away all my aches.
When then I became a better person, only because I knew I could be.
Just had to wake up and admit the fact that this is but a dream.
Awake now, you see, this reality is nothing more than a dream.

170

Faith Holds Me Cold

Faith holds me cold, I am a bastard indeed.
Judge me once more, my cynical friend.
Do your best to chop me to the knee.

God holds me screaming, Mother I feel like I cannot awake.
This nightmare is now choking, around my throat like a snake.
Hope has me dying, wishing that I could reach.
Faith holds me cold, as my life becomes weak.

So step now on further, upon the road of truth.
Judge me again you predictable fuck, yes it's true that I am the Devil.
Faith holds me cold, here at the end of what God wanted of me.
Faith holds me cold, please Mother wake me, I cannot breathe.

Can't Resist

Sorry bitch I just can't resist.
At least I admit that I am son of a bitch.
So shut the fuck up and get on your knees.
I just can't resist, when you get your wish.
There you are smiling on your knees.

Sorry bitch, but I must tell you that I don't give a damn today.
Go ahead and do as you wish, waste your time and slap my face.
Give back that in which you feel that you have taken of me.
I just can't resist shutting you up, while you're on your knees.

It does help to have a nice cold drink.
Can't resist to just letting it all go, and enjoy sweet release.
Just shut the fuck up, I don't need this nonsense anymore.
I very much do love it, when after she is done.
How she is a little bit less of a bore.

A Touch Of Amber

It doesn't hurt just to add a touch of Amber.
Then all secure reason begins to feel shocked.
The hallway is truly endless for years now we've been lost.
No way now to end the chatter, it tastes so sweet with *a touch of Amber.*

All has been great up to this point, but a backlash I fear.
I don't want to look down right now, I do know what I will see.
That I have stepped over the ledge, and I am falling.
One more touch of Amber, then I will accept this dream.

It doesn't hurt to just lean over and kiss her goodnight.
Still I wonder if she will remember, now that it is *the middle of the night.*
The hallway is endless, and I fear that *there is somebody following behind me.*
One last touch of Amber, and I believe now that we are ready.

This Knight's War

For years now upon the roads, this soldier marches on.
For I have a promise in which I must never break.
I must move on further, for there is more war to wage.
For so many years past, oceans of blood seeped into the dirt.
Was once a man of honor, now ash to ash and memories to fade.
This knight has progressed, to a state of true honor.
Either dragged upon the road with worn down boot and sole.
Or carried gently upon the cradle of rose petals and fall leaves.
This war must wage on, for there are still evils in which must pay.
There are many more demons, still yet to stand in my way.
For so many years now, upon this road towards my one true love.
I will come home, I must return, but there is still war to be fought.
Never seems to end, and again this knight's blade separates flesh.
And blood rains a light mist from the sky, another pawn thrown away.
Still I must fight my way, to rest in the arms of my one true love.
This knight's war will never end, until all battles are won.

"I will return home to you..."

Plastered To the Floor

Passion rings numb as I am plastered to the floor.
The moon's tears drip off my teeth, then tear reality away.
I dance with the ashes of a corpse, she does know what I mean.
Again, I'm plastered to the floor, staring into my own face.

Can rip and tear the logic, aside gone and tormented through time.
Can't bear to stand your neglect, truly you are a bitch indeed.
And from where I lie, I just cannot see, here plastered on the floor.
From then my throat, the smoke does bleed, no I cannot be saved.

Passion rings numb as then my mind is grinded against the stone.
The zombie weeps sad tears of tar, as God and the Devil stand alone.
I can't help but to punish, myself for having no soul.
Lying here plastered to the floor, we know now there is no hope.

Earthquake In My Soul

She whispered once softly, that I was her dream.
At one point she must have awakened, and then erased me.
I tried my best to be there, and catch her as she fell.
I was one moment too late, then I woke in Hell.

An earthquake in my soul, I feel as if I've been cursed.
That would make a little sense, but I will not get off that easy.
And yes the Devil has a hold of me, because I don't give a damn.
Yes all the angels weep for me, then again I am burnt away...

On that day she whispered softly, those poetic rhymes into me.
At one point I had died, when she slit her wrist because of me.
I feel now that I could take it, and admit that I am fucked.
An earthquake in my soul, so I guess now I am out of luck.

Does No One See?

Does no one see, does no one see, what is killing me?
I am ready now to eat the flesh of any bastard that stands in my way.
Just ready now, yes ready now, to take one more step.
Then very gently the blade is slid across all enemy throats.
This is not a joke, this is not a joke, you are all fucking dead…

Lying On a Cloud

Here lying on a cloud as watching the world just drift by.
True apathy has been found today, so I let out a gentle sigh.
All seems to be right in place, all the gears collectively turning.
Here lying on a cloud, just laughing as the world drifts on by.

There they go, dancing away, all the angels of the past.
True apathy will never be cast away, again *I no longer seem to give a damn.*
All seems to be right in place, here as I lie on this cloud.
The world, it just drifts on by, on this beautiful pointless day.

Cynical Divide

There you stand, my cynical friend, it sure has been some time.
Great to see you once again, but it's not the same as last time.
When once I was there to catch you right before the ground you hit.
Now the tables have turned, and you are left alone waist deep in shit.

Such a cynical divide, you went your way and I went mine.
Great to see that you're happy now, alone you ponder *"what if…"*
It is so sad to see now, you so deep in your own shit.
But I had to save myself, before the ground I did hit.

There you are my cynical friend, egotistical to the very end.
It is so great to see that you have let all of your dreams just fade and die.
Maybe we should just give it time, but it seems to me a waste.
I apologize not, for the cynical divide.
"Fuck you and all your games…"

Chapter *10*

Porcelain-Doll Screams

Pretentious

You love to paint the surface, of these hallways that we walk.
You love to preach your nonsense, upon these ears your words are lost.
You want to be an idol, the star in which all will blindly follow.
You truly are pretentious, such a predictable disgrace.

You wish to be the answer, to the logic for all our mistakes.
You love to push your nonsense, six feet deeper beyond the grave.
You take all that the weaker give you, with a smile and a wink.
Such a pretentious waste of nonsense, now to us so very bleak.

I have tried my best to restrain this, I believe now I'm going to snap.
I've done my best to help you, now a mistake I must correct.
I will eventually stop you, you and all of your pathetic bullshit.
You are so fucking pretentious, it truly makes me sick.

Degeneration

All fades back and seems unclear.
A looming picture of those past years.
Yes, there it waits hanging above the stairs.
Pain burning so cold, and I seem not to care.

Left judged and admitted to the jest.
The earthworm smiles, bleeding acid off its fang.
These eyes roll back, upon thousands of yesterdays.
It must be true, that I wish not to be saved.

Her once beautiful smile, memories burnt into my mind.
It all begins to disintegrate, erased but I feel fine.
Yes, there is a better way, to smile as stepping over the ledge.
All fades back and seems unclear.
The grim truth, that tomorrow we cannot save.

Thriving Virus

Walking through the woods one snowy evening.
I felt as if I was being watched.
Walking through the woods one snowy evening.
I could not shake the feeling that I was being stalked.

Marching through a pasture one snowy evening.
The moon shining full in the beautiful starlit sky.
Marching through a pasture one snowy evening.
There was something behind me, a fact I could not deny.

Running through a field one snowy evening.
I could feel the monster biting at my heels.
Running through a field one snowy evening.
The monster took hold of me, and sank its teeth into my neck.

Returning to the woods one snowy evening.
I felt as if I was one with nature.
Returning to the woods one snowy evening.
The virus thrives, and I am now alive.

Thunder & Smiles

The child known as God is weeping now.
Lightning and thunder reaching across the sky.
The child known as God is angry.
We have failed his once beautiful dream.

Acid rains from the sky.
Beautiful blue rose petals begin to fill the air.
The lonely child known as the Devil.
He smiles now, because all is clear.

The pointless sheep.
Known as the humanity, in which plagues this world.
The thunder it grows louder.
So smile now all, for this is the end today.

The Omega

Reach your hand into the sky.
Grab the stars and pull them down.
Reach your hand into my chest.
It is only poisonous tar that you pull out.

Look beyond the murder.
See that she was a beautiful woman.
Tear beyond the logic.
Admit to yourself, that you are insane.

Fall behind your conscious.
Cut into the middle, it is laughter thriving inside.
Smile as the atom bombs fall.
The omega calls, now we are home.

RollerCoaster

My eyes have seen.
Then left abandoned at the start.
My heart it dreams.
No more time left to heal these scars.

My flesh it is weeping.
Torn back further to reveal the truth.
My mind it is creeping.
Deeper into the abyss known as sanity.

The rollercoaster is rushing.
Deeper it digs into my past.
I cannot deny this any longer.
For the truth is, that we are never coming back.

My eyes they have seen.
Then left discarded at the first step.
At the peak now, then the rollercoaster begins to fall.
Twisting off the track, we all scream and we all laugh.
I cannot deny this any longer, the fact that we can never go back.

Injecting More

The needle pushes harder against the middle of my throat.
A slight shock as it penetrates the skin.
Then forcefully all of the relentless acid is injected within.
Seeping so very deep into my once blissful mind.

I am injecting more.
Just to push myself over the edge.
I am screaming louder.
So does it feel not the same as back then?

I was a greater logic.
Now I am just a fucking piece of trash.
I did hold love in my heart once.
But now I have moved on, because she is dead.

The needle is broken off under the flesh in the middle of my throat.
Still I wish for you to inject more, to get me passed today.
For I was once a fighter, ready to find a better way.
Come on now and inject more, so I can awake somewhere in the past.
A place where she is still waiting, she's still waiting, still waiting.
As so fucking pathetically I am still injecting more...

Translucent

Once upon a twisted shallow day.
I was the child that told God.
"I do believe that I shall never be saved."
As once left up to the killer behind the drape.
All was sadly taken and violently raped away.
For I am a ghost, here screaming in front of your face.
I am a demon, here weeping behind this very page.
I am translucent, left discarded in the back.
I was once a part of your life, now lost in the past.
I have tried my best to be there, yet I could not reach.
I did try to warn you, now your bones begin to freeze.
I was the child that once told God.
"I will be forever, always the ghost that remains lost..."

Tell Me I Was Real.

Come on baby and tell me I was real.
Right before we pull the trigger.
Our castle in the sand is gone and washed away.
Come on baby and tell me I was real.
As we watch all the colors, one by one begin to fade.

Reach right inside and take whatever is left.
Bleed a river into the circle.
Neon clouds of smoke bleeding off our breath.
So tell me I was real and that I mean something more.
Right before we pull the trigger.
Turn off the lights and let us but sing along.

Come on now my love and let us laugh.
As all that once held meaning, it has collapsed.
These teeth are breaking, grinding against the bone.
I do not want to feel so very cold and alone.
So come on please and tell me I was real.
Then we pull the trigger and all is calm…

Unexplored Terrain

I just can't explain where it is that I'm standing at this time.
The sky radiating a pale green, *golden clouds circling around*.
Red lightning exploding out and reaching from horizon to horizon.
I just don't understand where it is that I am standing today.

This truly is an unexplored terrain.
The ground is made of broken glass and burning coals.
Ash fills my lungs, as the temperature is growing so very cold.
Where am I standing now, in this odd world?

I just can't grip it right, the fact that I must be lost.
Here where no man has ever stepped foot.
It is so very strange indeed, being misplaced somewhere in hell.
This world is unexplored, and God has left it all to me…

No Parachute...

Our left engine is out now.
Captain can't hold us steady much longer.
The right engine is dead.
Losing altitude and speed.
Have no choice but to abandon.
Women and children first.
The cabin is on fire.
All we can hear now is muffled screams.

Beginning now a downward spiral.
Almost all passengers have escaped.
Still many lie dead in the aisles.
The horizon is gone.
Now out of time.
So we jump, pure panic and hysterical screams.
Then realizing there is no parachute.
So I smile, as downward I proceed.
"Ain't that a bitch?"

Sphere

Was faded and stretched across the lines of faith.
A red mark across the throat.
She was the right words that I could not speak.
Then I knew the bitter truth.

As lusted harder against.
Then all at once the emotions were raped.
Held against our will in terror.
It makes no sense, that today we would return...

Was tedious and left bleeding at the door to the church.
Now all seems so beautifully distorted.
As at the dawn now of the true end of me.
Then once more the sphere turns.
Bringing me back all the truths I hate of me...

Stepping Over a Corpse

I can't do it now, I can't do it now.
I need to breathe, I need to breathe.
I can't save us now, I can't save us now.
The lights are off, now through the darkness the monster can see.

I want it more, I want it more!
I need to scream, I need to scream!
The answers corrupted, the answers corrupted.
Mother Earth is dead, for as of today we shall never be free...

I won't let it go, I won't let you go.
I need to just breathe, I need to just breathe.
I can't correct it now, I can't protect you now.
You are dead and as I step over your corpse.
"I hope that you may someday forgive me..."

At Least I Tried!

At least I tried and gave it my best.
Only to sadly fail us both at the end.
At least I tried to stop you that day.
From walking out and leaving us in pain.

All answers have been questioned.
All questions deeply considered.
At least I tried to be there.
But you were comfortable and did not care.

It was a fucked up act that ended in blood and tears.
It was the moon that was there to shine me light.
You were such an interesting creature.
At least I tried to prove my love.

All answers have been discarded.
All questions now relapse again and again.
Only to illustrate this poet as a twisted man.
But at least I tried to say that I cared.
At least I said I loved you, *as you took my last breath of air...*

Little Sweet Angel

My little sweet angel, can you reach my hand.
Take me high to the heaven skies.
To prove that God will both deny me and cast me out.
Oh please my little sweet angel, I need this today.

As countlessly gyrating and smashing against the walls of the endless hallway.
There are no more secrets left but the one.
A downright despicable truth I do hate.
Then open the bottle, drink it down, for it is far too late.

My little sweet angel, so heavenly you dance before my eyes.
To entertain and educate, singing as you dance upon the thin red line.
And at once the rusted bloody tar rises up and out.
It is steaming, rotten lumps of human flesh.

My little sweet angel, can you reach me from there.
Here in this sanitarium I lay awake so blissfully drugged.
As repeatedly I can't help but to smash the brick against my skull.
My love, take my hand, *"for right now I feel so very cold…"*

Holistic Rush

It's over, still over and waiting on credits.
It's colder, much colder and we cannot deny it.
It's not there, but somewhere – still hollow.
We've been there, and seen it – the dreams of the monster.

Some time, a pointless rhyme.
As beneath the ocean can either of us breathe?
No tricks, now so sick.
It is today in which we shall burn the cradle.

We're over, still over and waiting on nothing.
It's burning, not learning and we wish only to escape it.
We're rushing, all rushing towards the back of our sanity.
We've been there, and seen it – *"the end that is yet to be."*

184

Divine We Perceive

Speak to me my Lord, of that which resides beyond the stars.
Drip the acid down, it rains neon into my eyes.
Speak to me my one true God from your heart.
As divine we perceive, that there is at this time no more hope.

Give to me my Devil, the true evil that I deserve.
Then she runs her tongue across my ear.
Give to me my Devil, no better lesson to learn.
As beyond all logic, now remains only pain and fear.

Try to cut into it, the mind of the lonely freak.
Try to burn whatever you don't understand.
And you do know that I mean but only me…
Speak now to me with your own true voice my lord.
Then divine we shall perceive.

Colliding Convictions

It makes no sense to me, but then again I am insane.
I am out there right now dancing on the moon.
Even though I'm right here in front of your face.
Just pointing out the facts that you wish not to see.

As blind now as ever, we are but worthless swine.
As drugged up like always, I'm beginning to feel fine.
It makes no sense to me, but I really just don't care.
So fuck it all, and let us smile as we enter despair.

It makes you look like the whore that you are.
So hold tight onto that pointless bastard's arm.
It makes me feel sick now, every time I see your face.
It makes no sense and I love that, and I'm glad it hasn't changed.

As torn down like so many years ago, far back in the past.
All our beliefs held meaning but now are but only trash.
You were once a queen in my eyes, now you truly are a whore.
It makes a little more sense as now I see, from behind that open door…

Bio-Weapon

I am a fucking bio-weapon.
I am the death of this perverse world.
You are the answer that was never given.
You are the coldness of this hollow void.

For I am a true bio-weapon.
An epidemic infesting the human soul.
You are the once meaningful notion.
The cure to the virus known today as Me...

I am a fucking psycho killer.
I will eat at your flesh as you watch in fear.
You cannot stop me, you cannot run.
You my porcelain doll can only scream.

Four Letter Word

Far too many years have passed through these eyes.
Un-known of the curse my heart cannot hide.
Call me a demon for I truly am.
Kill me now my love, then burn my ashes again.

Lost everything that I once loved right at the start.
Over so many years, I have misplaced some scars
Violently the pain returns, reminding me who I am
Everything that I hold is the same, just fucking dead.

Far too many skeletons hidden within my head.
Un-knowing of the truth that my heart has died.
Can ever there be a chance for some hope to live?
Kill me please my love before I open my eyes.

Lost everything all over again and it is just the same.
Over so many long years I have fought it.
Violently you my love have cut off this poet's face.
Eternally now and always, we are the ones that made this game.

Cotton Candy

"Hello........" *I think that I might be too late?*
Where did everyone go? "Please my loves don't hide from me."
Goddamn it's fucking cold, *here below the dirt as I wait!*

Where does the pain go?
When it starts to crack the bone.
Laughing so hard as my childhood self throws the pills back at me...
Regurgitating up the stars into the night sky.
Somewhere into the middle of a desert.
That is the place where I will play out my inevitably.
So very sweet, as the cotton candy LSD bleeds inside.

"Hello........" *Is anyone else home or is it just me?*
Shit! I think that I fell off and into another rant...
Gone beyond any form of logic, and I'm not coming back.
So where does all the pain go?
When the cotton candy flavored death is injected into the bone.
We awake alive, right out side of our sanity...

Drone

Lead me on into her arms.
Let her rip away my flesh.
Lead me far beyond the dawn.
Let her have me and all that's left.

Lust me great into the past.
Time has stopped but it will not last.
Shove your hand in, into my brain.
Eat it all to understand what I say.

Fuck me good and let us scream.
As I shove my dick inside.
So very intense we both scream.
Together our bodies writhe.

Lead me deep into her thoughts.
Let me stay and become forever lost.
Lead me not back into the clear.
I am hers now and to the very end.

Flames Beneath My Feet

Race me to the other side of the nightmare.
As falling down, I weep because I am weak.
Take me back to my childhood.
A tormented hell, burning flames beneath my feet.

Judge me God, for I am a demon with angel wings.
Hold me closer my love, I am afraid of the dark.
This jail is locked, I am a freak in a cage.
Left alone in hell, and it's all still the same.

Wake me when we arrive at the other side of then.
Shake me hard, beat me as hard as you physically can.
Am I not going to wake from this nightmare tonight?
But I am awake, and this hell is my life.

So race me far beyond to the other side of the moon.
As falling out of my bed, out of my head.
Upon the lips of the demon waits mankind's assured doom.
So I weep because I am alone, I am weak.
Here in my own hell, eternal flames beneath my feet.

Between the Thin Lines

Between the thin lines hidden is all that was real.
Left to be the sick little child, with wounds that cannot be healed.
Beaten and scared, there in the cold dark – "back-room."
Between the thin lines, still remains our once hidden truth.

From behind the eyelids rushing, the bitter knowledge we fear.
Silver injected into the veins, and we cannot be saved this time.
So get us there into the clear, taken far beyond the rhyme.
For none now to say, who is left alive.

Beaten so brutal, scars remain and remind us of the past.
That dark shattered echo, a haunting memory that remains.
So taken far where we cannot see, somewhere lost in time.
And the truth remains hidden, between the thin red lines.

Syringe

As once embraced and left in the past.
I held her beautiful face within my so very cold hands.
There was a question lingering upon the situation.
But the doctors inject and reality is no more.

At one time we were so very perfect.
And were meant to be together until the end of time.
Then at once it all came to an abrupt ending.
Then I opened my eyes to see that I am blind.

For one divine sacrifice given.
Then the Devil knows that I am calling his name.
As once I did love her until the end of all that is to be.
So I guess now that all is over.
Erased and now but only a fragmented porcelain doll scream.

Backwards Smiles...

Can one achieve, that dire simple fact?
In the middle of the frozen lake, waits a rusted and bloodstained ax.
For not to be remembered.
Only a skipped chapter within this relentless tome.
Still backwards smiles hang about.
Proving the truth that in this darkness I am alone.

Can then our flesh sustain the flames?
Or are we all just leaping over the edge with a smile.
Then can there be a chance for freedom?
Or is this all that is left of our world?
I fear that I will never truly know.
Just what it is that has driven this mind insane.

So can no one achieve it, that truly grim fact?
Is there a better way to explain all of this?
I need to let the guilt go because it is all my fault.
Still here in my torment, this distorted world remains the same.
All around me lingers backwards smiles.
This world is dead, and we are the same...

Elevate

Can't look now, so cut out your fucking eyes.
Can't feel now, I think that my heart has died.
Can't even begin to call myself human any more.
Can't believe that we've come this far and still so much more.

We won't be there to see it, the saving of yesterday.
We won't be there to feel it, the triumph of today.
We won't be there to grasp it, the end of space and time.
We won't live to tell it, the beauty that tomorrow holds.

Death of the human soul and that which was once me.
Death speaks so numb and cold this winter of insanity.
Death holds it all and that shall remain until the very end.
Death is the only answer, eyes closed and now you see.

Reach Me

Mother, can you reach me from the other side of this page?
My love, can you save me from being erased?
God, can you kill me please if I ask real nice?
Please somebody reach me, and tell me that I'm going to be fine.

Mother can you wake me, from this damned eternal dream?
My love must you hate me, for I am but only a waste.
God can you forgive me, for taking that step deeper into hell?
Please somebody kill me, for I am just too overwhelmed.

Mother, can you hear me screaming on the other side of this page?
My love, can you please just admit that we don't want to be saved.
God you are a monster, laughing as we the world all burn.
Please *Oh* please somebody reach me, so that one of us might learn…

No Reply

Out there into the darkness I am screaming.
Can no one hear all my pain filled cries?
Out there into the shadows I am screaming.
And still to this day no one has replied.

Deep here within the ending.
The answers are burning and will soon be ash.
The mushrooms are dancing and singing their little songs.
As far through the unknown we venture on and on.

Out there into the darkness I am screaming.
Can no one hear as I so painfully shout and cry?
Out there into the shadows where I was created.
Still I receive no reply.

For ages of twisted poetic nonsense twirling within my brain.
I laugh while screaming at the mirror.
So I do believe that today the emotions remain the same.
As for so very long I have reached out there into the night.
Still here for so many ages, and no reply.
No reply...

Take the Helm

A step a little closer.
A mind a little bleak.
A death a little filtered.
And that is what's left of me.

A way a bit more to go.
A life's story yet to unfold.
A reason that never had a reason to be.
That is what was left here inside of me.

A truth a little hard to swallow.
A smoke filling these tired lungs.
An answer that was never given.
Now take the helm and let us make haste...

Chapter 11

A Bitter Design

Lingering Impressions

On turns the world and I think it's fading.
On burns the light and we want just to break it.
Then bleeds the turmoil that is flooding this head.
On goes the screaming, there hidden under my bed.

Then was taken so much deeper.
Beyond the murder of the child that never was.
As for so many ages.
Then bleeds the ashes and she was such a whore.
For nothing at this moment we need to endure.
Then taken so far passed the nonsense.
Into a life that is no more.

On turns the world and I believe it is ending.
On burns the fire and it won't soon be extinguished.
Then bleeds so much of the chatter that is flooding this head.
On lingers those impressions, far beyond life and into death.

Pull the Switch

Ready now, then pull the switch.
Forget me now, that is what you wish.
It's over now, but only a little more.
Into this chapter, of a bitter design.

Take us there to the other side.
Leave us dead and out of time.
We are nothing now and never was.
So pull the switch, as all comes undone.

So ready now to take that last step
It's over now so let us release our breath.
Beneath the waves so very far.
It is time to go, so now we depart...

Dive-Bomb

Head right for it.
Let out and watch it burn.
Hold onto both handles.
Fuck – we never learned.

Rip away at the logic.
Cut now deeper below the flesh.
Take now as it's steaming.
Do it now and eat it fresh.

Pull back against the moment.
Set aside all that made us real.
Pain of now you can take it.
There on top of that distant hill.

Reach right in and hold it.
That was once not the truth.
Jump right over and say just fuck it!
Now pull the pin and try to take some with you.

Subversive

I will soon stand and take control.
Of this world of weak pitiful wastes of flesh.
I will soon stand and laugh in your face.
For the sad truth is that we're both dead.

Here wandering lost in someone else's head.
That is the grim fate in which we now live.
But I will soon rise and then take control.
For I am the correct answer in which you seek.

I will not stop now, here at the end.
I will not break now, not the same as back then.
I will take control now, so open your eyes.
I am alive now, I am your conscious in which you try to deny.

Never She Did Exist

Was my heart that was breaking.
Was my mind that was hating.
As the darkness was growing.
As the end was still showing.

Then led afar and into the reality of today.
Dug deeper into the center, of this now demonic brain.
For maybe there was an answer to the question unasked.
If ever this story was real, I wish not to look back.

For she was so great then, my one true love.
For she was an angel, sent from above.
I was a nonentity that remains now, for that was her wish.
I would still love her if I could, but never she did exist…

Eternal Plunge

All set now, so I begin to lean over the edge.
Looking so far down, I cannot see an end.
Time now for me to step over the ledge.
All is set now and this is the end.

I am now falling deep into the unknown.
"God, maybe someday I just might be missed."
I have completed all actions which needed to be done.
"I know that you hate it but I've had enough of this."

All set now, as I begin my eternal plunge into "somewhere."
Still at this time I hope only to find some release.
For I have had enough of this torment.
And still you laugh, but that only proves you never knew me.

Just a smile, as here I am taking my eternal plunge.
Into hell or heaven, but it really doesn't matter to me.
For I have been gone all my life, lost in my head.
So even if I have killed myself, *I can't destroy what was already dead.*
"So only a smile and now forever I fall…"

Frantic & Flushed

All seems so very frantic and flushed.
As there you stand in front of me.
All seems so frantic and flushed.
As there you hold your blade so deep in my heart.

Come laugh with me, laugh with me, all the way into hell.
All has become so weak, we are so weak, now so overwhelmed.
I am a monster now, a demon now, wanting to see the light.
You are the Devil now, you are my Devil now, nothing but a waste.

All seems so very frantic and flushed.
As you stare so deeply into my eyes.
All seems so frantic and flushed.
For I did have a point once, but now I have died…

Stale Page

The sad truth is that I want to escape.
Please get me out before it's too late.
The sad truth is that I just want to be free.
But I'll never live to see beyond today.

Please get me out so I can say that I was there.
Please kill me now to end my despair.
Please just break me down until nothing is left.
Burn me away and now I'm but ash.

I am this stale page that still lingers on.
I am the true ache that you feel in your heart.
You are the reflection of this poet with no face.
You are the true reason, for all my endless pain.

Come on and forget me now before God can see.
Burn us away and say it was a dream.
Cut and tear until there is nothing else left.
We are the stale page, burning away and soon to be ash.

On the Road Again...

As on the road again, heading toward the end.
What was it truly that we once said?
Muffled and I cannot make it out, through all the noise.
As on the road again, wishing to erase our sins.

Dying for a chance and it never arrives.
Maybe this is but a dream, so we open our eyes.
Only to see the long road that still lies ahead.
I don't know where I'm going, here on the road again.

As on the road I weep, haunted by yesterday.
Tell me why has tomorrow not come, maybe I'll just wait.
Here on the road again, I know that I might soon reach an end.
So I keep moving forward, beyond all our sins.

As into hell I stroll, knowing I will never return.
What was it my love, that you had said on that day.
Maybe this is but a dream, and I'm just fighting to awake.
Here on the road again, the endless road of leaves...

Chemical Burns

Tell me now, what did mother say.
Kill me now, then throw my worthless body away.
I am a pointless jest, still hoping to be more.
I am the truth, hidden behind the open door.

Tell me now, what the fuck did you say!?
Kill me please, then erase my useless name.
It is futile I believe, but you don't seem to care.
You are the relentless poison, filling the cool night air.

Chemical burns now covering all of my body.
So I scream laughing because this is what I wanted.
To be just murdered, for I am but a waste.
God tell me now before all of this is over.
"What did mother say!?"

Weapon Of Choice

This mind has been shattered.
Then spread all across the universe.
This heart has been raped and beaten.
Then all at once this world began to die...

Rushing waves of flame, flood all the streets.
An end now beginning to shine a better way.
All that is left is nonsense, so yes it is the same.
And there will be no better outcome, only an Armageddon.

This mind has been shattered.
Then spread all across the universe.
This heart was taken and then left in shame.
All that I once loved, it's all been taken away.

Rushing waves of flame, flooding within my thoughts.
Troubled notions of now you are sorry and all is lost.
So grab now your one weapon of choice.
For the end has come and now it begins...

When I Didn't Care

When I thought I cared, I just laughed as I watched you fall.
When I wasn't there, it was always me you did mock.
Behind my back, you were so twofaced when I wasn't near.
So I had but only to laugh, back when I thought I cared.

There was a time when we were both happy.
So very ready and willing to rise and seize the day.
But it must have been all just another awkward dream.
Just like this one in which I've lived for so many years.

It reminds me of a time when I tried my best to be there.
At your side to keep you safe no matter what strives I must bear.
It all reminds me of a time, so very many past years.
A time when we were happy, "a time when I didn't care..."

Knock On Wood

Can't force it out, then the lines break.
All the evil in me, now it has escaped.
The time to leave a meaning has already passed.
So knock on wood, but that won't save you this time.

It came to be a nonsense we hate.
Now all that is left is for us to let it go.
Tomorrow has been taken away.
But at least we can say we had the nerve to try.

We can't stop it now, the truth it bleeds out.
Evil it makes me whole, for I am but a demon.
The time to make amends is now sadly passed.
Knock on wood if you wish, but it will not protect you this time.

Sideways

Such a strange viewpoint that keeps one aware.
At the edge of this sanity, all fades now bleak.
Then into the last of our travesties, and we shall not tell.
It is left now within, upon the very last level of hell.

Such a demonic characteristic, parading about before the mirror.
At the edge of the blade all now seems so much clearer.
Then into the brimful river of blood and a relentless ash.
It is true what they say, that we are never coming back.

Such a twisted conviction now pressed against ones will.
At the edge of the cliff now and it is time to let go.
The one last time upon the grim action of sweet bitter dismay.
It is that which we had always feared, felt deep within.

Such a fucked up sideways point of view one can no longer deny.
At the end now of this sanity, and I don't even care why.
Then into not so much of a superior driving notion of blissful faith.
It is the true end now of our sanities, left here completely sideways…

The Zombie's Tome

For so many ages, here waiting six feet below.
For so many troubles, here etched in this endless tome.
For there was an answer but none were strong enough to find.
We had once seen the face of God, but then we went blind.

This zombie has risen, to try and correct so many misdeeds.
Then without a chance, all had turned such a darker shade of gray.
For there is no chance to save this soul, it is already gone.
But I will live forever, and always known as the eternally damned.

Yes I once was a human, I had tried to live a life of grace.
But I was murdered, because I did believe in so much more.
I was a poet, damned to forever live out this endless rhyme.
I am now and forever shall be the zombie, here locked within this tome.

For so many ages, saving all the relentless chronicling of this tormented being.
For so many troubles, resting upon the shoulders of the weak.
For there was once a noble poet, that wished only to give hope.
Now I am forever the damned zombie, left behind to fill this endless tome.

Fucking Twisted

Fucking twisted, lying here.
Living lies, of what you always hear.
Of what to do beyond disorder.
The mission aborted, mangled-distorted, faith fucking morbid.

As fucking hating this life and her.
Left trying and frying, I feel the burn.
Come now show me - give me - I know that's it!
The fading smoke within our endless abyss.

Fucking twisted, crying here.
Living the lie that we always feared.
Now what to do beyond disorder…
The mission aborted, we cannot afford it, now faith fucking morbid.

Twilight Sorrow

Naught felt as such a nicer sense of dying hope.
Then upon all the twilight sorrows we all begin to choke.
With those now unexplainable moments of our past.
We have only today to see how it will end.

For that to be left only for the Devil to hold.
All the bitter nonsense that floods this aching mind.
The war has taken over but again I think I'll be fine.
Just knowing now that in the end only the twilight sorrows shall remain.

The Ghost That Remains

Must now admit, that I am the ghost that remains.
Must now be sick, as it comes up once again.
It burns like fire, as then watching the blood come out.
It is now over, but still a little more remains.

Must now admit, that I am but only a sideshow freak.
Must now just stop, then get the fuck away from me.
It is a fact that you are a filthy little creature from hell.
It is so true, that I am a ghost, remaining here, for only you…

Mirrors Melting

It is so beautiful, as watching the mirrors melting.
It is so great, knowing that we are all dead.
It is so haunting, the face of a love that I did erase.
It's just so damn beautiful, watching everything burn to ash.

You were my love once, when I was truly me.
You were my only chance, of ever setting my heart free.
So yesterday was the dying, of all that I once held.
So today I just smile, as watching the mirrors melt.

"Here so deep in our own personal hell."

As Sanity Becomes a Dream

Just have to laugh as sanity becomes a dream.
Just have to laugh because we were never free.
We all tried and failed to save our mortal souls.
It's just so funny, that we will never fully see.

Just have to cry as sanity becomes but a dream.
Just have this now, the pain that was forcefully pushed upon me.
We all wanted to be there, to see the other side.
Sanity then spoke, and now we know we were never really alive.

Mother Was Sad

Mother was sad, when she called and no one answered.
Mother tried her best but no one ever replied.
Mother was sad, when she tried her best to get there.
Mother couldn't make it, there was just not enough time.

Mother was angry, and said things she didn't mean to say.
Mother tried to say she was sorry, but the line just went dead.
Mother was sad, when she called and no one answered.
Mother is crying, for the line is dead and can never be fixed...

I Fall - Again...

I fall again, in hopes that tomorrow might be saved.
I fall again, into this abyss that I chose for me.
I want this to pass, so I can just let go.
I want the sun to rise, and melt away all the snow.

I fall again, into the darkness of this twisted mind.
I fall again, into the shadows of a much darker time.
I want you to be there, to say that I meant so much more.
I fall again, in the hopes that I just might hit the floor.

"To free me now from myself."

Pursuing the Truth

All through the darkness, I am pursuing the truth.
I don't think I'll ever find it, and neither will you.
All for better reasons, and we need not to show them today.
It has been so very long and still has yet to change.

All through the darkness, I am trying to find a better way.
I don't believe I'll ever find it, so all hope is lost.
I do know now that this is the outcome, for all of our sins.
It is time now to let go, so come follow me once again.

All through the darkness, I am pursuing the truth.
All of my time now, has been wasted on you.
I don't want to be here, but I can never leave.
I see now the truth, and I shall keep it all to me…

Answers With Dust

God and the Devil have spoken.
They have left their message in the dust.
We cannot but on our own find it.
We must pray that someday we shall see.

God and the Devil have taken.
And then left their message deep in the ash.
We cannot today just reach it.
We must wait and hope to see the end.

Humanity it is failing and we are lost.
We have destroyed any chance of ever knowing why.
As God and the Devil have spoken their views of disgust.
They have left the answer for us to find.
Buried deep below the dust.

Covet

Hold onto me my dear.
I am that what you seek.
Hold on and just smile.
Let the passion take control.

Desire me my love.
For I am that what you seek.
Hold on and just let go.
So only passion shall remain.

Hold onto me my dear.
Then look deep into my eyes.
Tell me I was real.
Just before you turn on the lights.

Demonic Thoughts Creeping

As again this soul is fleeting, such demonic thoughts creeping.
I wonder if I felt it leaving, all the emotions screaming.
As onto the concert bleeding, all notions left weeping.
I know that we were dreaming, such demonic thoughts creeping.

A mind torn on the edge of reality, this is truly my fate.
A world left gone and buried, hidden deep in shame.
There was a path that was given, but then we turned around.
To take back what made us real, and then cast it out.

As again this soul is fleeting, with such sorrow reaping.
I wonder it I knew you were leaving, all emotions weeping.
As onto the paper sheet it was seeping, such demonic thoughts creeping.
And I do know that this tired soul shall never be saved.

Smash Until Gone

Say you'll be there and it won't take long.
Say that you really cared, and then just sing along.
Say that I was a riddle, unable to be completed.
Say that you loved me, and death was but a dream.

Smash it against the logic of what was not real.
Obtained over the violence, hidden on-top that hill.
Speak not for the reasons, as pain still stands firm.
Smash until gone, and hope to someday learn.

Say that you'll be there, and it won't take long.
Say that you really cared, and you will sing along.
Say that I was a nonsense, unable to be misplaced.
Say that you truly loved me, and then burn me away…

Come Dying

Come dying and signify one's self as our legitimacy.
Push the nail in place and watch as the mushrooms scream.
Rub your tongue against the grain and see what I know.
Fuck all that was known as reason, for we are surely alone.

Come dying my love and take me deep into your arms.
Push then the notion that we are but only a fragment of a shard.
Then led afar unto the philosophies of the grim that is.
Absent now in the eyes that hold over and prove so clearly the jest.

Come dying and establish one's self as our legitimacy.
Place the nail within and writhe as all the little mushrooms scream.
Pour the LSD onto your eyes, so maybe then you could see.
Fuck all that was once known as reason, for we are far passed the end.
"Come dying into a life, inevitable as it surely stands…"

Lost My Mind / Found My Heart

I lost my mind yet found my heart.
I am frozen now and full of tar.
It was a better loss of today it is so.
I lost my mind yet found my heart, there deep below the ocean of snow.

I was a demon that wished for light.
I was a dreamer that never slept at night.
I was a lover that just wished for love.
I was a hero, but today I am dust.

I lost my mind yet found my heart.
I am a hollow shell just torn apart.
It was a better thought then of maybe so.
I lost myself out there, so deep below the relentless snow.

For I was a demon there standing with angel wings.
I was a dreamer living out all of his endless dreams.
I was a fighter that had to fight every day.
I lost my mind yet found my heart, *when I admitted that you were but a dream.*

Megalomaniacal

I am the reason that is flowing just beneath your flesh.
I am your reflection and every educated guess.
I was your feelings when you said that you didn't have them.
I was your God then, the drug in which you craved.
I am the common sense infesting all of your brain.
I am the ongoing torment, in which you'll forever hate.
I am the voice that is right now screaming inside your head.
I am the thing you fear the most, the monster under your bed.
I will be now and always the thing that creeps within.
I will be there hidden, to justify every pointless sin.
For you cannot deny me, the one whom rules your thoughts.
Here within your head, I am the Devil and I am your God.
Left to stand as the only reason, hidden within your skull.
I am the one that controls you, for I am your thriving soul…

Chapter 12

Vanished Child

Storm In a Shallow Bottle

The stage is calling, and I'm ready to go home.
The end is coming, and they will all fear the truth.
An answer coming, that is what plagues my mind.
So all I have at this moment, is running out of time.

A storm in a shallow bottle, as I spin it tilted slightly on its side.
A tornado now growing, much more violent behind my eyes.
The accuracy has all ended, as have the concerns of that love.
Now I remember the truth again, "that I did never care…"

The stage is calling, and I must not disappoint.
The end is over, so just watch the snowflakes melt away.
It is all so bothered, the chronicles this soul has undergone.
So all I have at this moment, is just running out of time.

A storm in a shallow bottle, and then I smash it against my head.
Only in the hopes that I might for once just wake up dead.
For the truth is now infesting, my so very troubled mind.
The storm has calmed down now, and only blood can be seen...

I'd Rather Die!

I'd rather die, than admit defeat.
I'd rather die, then confirm your deceit.
I want to just fall, and watch the stars pass by.
I want to see the credits roll, then all goes dark.

I'd rather die, than admit that I did truly love you.
I'd rather die, and just let it all go.
I need just to focus, "Goddamn I'm high."
Tomorrow's gonna be a bitch, but I say bring it.

I'd rather die, than lose at this bet.
You cannot beat me, yes I'm talking to you "*Bitch*"…
I'd rather die, than admit that I will fail.
You cannot stop me, "Goddamn I'm on a roll."
No – you will not win...

Middle of The Page

Come see me now, become but a waste.
It all has passed and now again the rain begins to fall.
What is this nonsense, which is tearing inside of me?
Death now lingering as my shadow, this is what I've seen.

Come take me now, beyond the horizon.
Lead us then into the pains of so many tomorrows to come.
Then all pulled away, left at the middle of the page.
A shattered thought, still it haunts me.

As a dire whim, I did want to be the hero to save the day.
Yet I failed and then my whole world slipped away.
I've tried to tolerate the nonsense, all the childish games.
I am now but a shattered thought, left at the middle of the page.

Face Into the Ashes

Face into the ashes.
Bleed the sanity of all its sins.
Take shelter and hope they didn't see.
We must be silent, "they are here..."

Face against the moment.
Tear out the eyes, of that photo of then.
But all that's left is ashes and smoke yet again.
Leave behind nothing, for this is that fate.

Face into the ashes.
I believe that I am going to soon freak.
All is now waving, I think I'm gonna be sick.
The room it is spinning, I think that I might fall.

Face first into the ashes.
Head first falling against the stone.
I think that I'm gonna be sick.
Then it comes up and all over the floor...

You Were My Friend...

Once upon a time, you were my friend.
Once upon a time, we wished it never to end.
At one time then, we wished never to part.
But now passed the end, it was such a waste of time.

I wonder if I'll make it, and prove that I am just that good.
I feel like I've been tied down, and the ghost now touches my spine.
At one moment we were lost, somewhere deep in space.
The echoes are calling, repeating what they say.

Once upon a time you loved me, and I the same for you.
Once upon a time you did kill me, with your knife in my chest.
At one time we were lost in a labyrinth, unable to escape.
But then we opened our eyes, to see the end to be.

I wonder if I'll ever make it, and prove that I am truly me.
I feel that something great is coming, soothing upon a rebirth.
As once you and I were friends, but today that cannot be.
For I am dead and so are you, lost somewhere so deep in space.

Silence Stirs

Silence stirs behind her words.
Echoes fading long into the night.
For darkness blooms right here at noon.
Then reality is all taken away.

She is an angel with *such a beautiful face*.
Every time she speaks though, my heart breaks numb.
There is just something that sadly eats at me.
Maybe the fact that she is truly no angel indeed.

Silence stirs behind our words.
Echoes of screams ringing through the night.
For now as my hatred blooms, here presently at noon.
The reality is, that all has been taken away.

Follow the Commandments

Run all you little sheep.
Pointless little lambs to the slaughter.
Follow your Lord my beloved, and say all your prayers.

Keep pushing your relentless bullshit.
Pointless little views and no one cares.
Follow the commandments, to shelter your heart from despair.

Leap all you faithful believers.
Over the ledge and against the jagged stones.
Follow the word of the Lord, and question not his will.

Run all you little sheep.
Pointless little creatures jumping headfirst into your end.
Follow the commandments, to lead one's heart from sin...

A River of Blood

I have come far this time.
To reach the answers of how.
And I know that at times it doesn't make any sense.
But still I just let go and then follow through.

Then comes a rushing river of blood.
Flowing so violently from her wrist.
It is a true shock and she is getting pale.
She has to hold on, or she's not gonna make it.

I have come far this time.
I know that I have truly but just begun.
And I know that I will make it.
For I shall not drown, in this river the blood.

Ten Times More

Come on hit me ten times more.
Come on cut me and bring me to the floor.
Come on and break all of my bones.
Come hit me again ten times harder.
Then maybe you might leave a dent…

So We're the Same

So we're the same, just dreamers that think clear.
So we are the same, just wanting to escape this cage.
So we're the same, just killers that want to take control.
So we are the same, damned souls that shall never be saved.

So you are the cancer that is rotting my brain.
So you are the hatred that is still driving me.
So I am the logic that did sadly fail.
So I am the lost man, here wandering hell…
"So we are the same."

Push Me to the Brink

Push me further to the brink.
Watch then as the moon bleeds.
Taken so graceful from the starlit sky.
Ten million more reasons, of the notion why.

So push us then far beyond hell.
And laugh so hard as the Devil weeps.
Take out then your blade and slay the beast.
Open your eyes to know, you are now alive.

Push me further passed the brink.
Then step back as I begin to snap.
Take then all that was ever a part of me.
And push me so very far, passed the brink.

Accurate Nonsense

I was judged then, standing alone in court.
I am a murderer, indeed I deserve to be locked away.
The neon lights are bending, tracers echoing behind.
The nonsense now makes so much sense, "*you should give it a try.*"

As for at this moment all is fading.
But truth be told I don't know where to...
I just want to smile, as now our story will soon conclude.
And in the end all of the nonsense, made so much sense...

The Number 13

Twisting are the faces that won't ever let me rest.
Lost in some strange graveyard, misplaced in my own head.
The number it is calling, and I do want to reply.
I don't think I can hold on any longer, but it'll be okay.

They tell me just to let go and admit that I will fail.
I've already done been there before, and have returned.
So what the fuck does it matter, you don't believe I'll make it.
But you must know that this poet can never be beaten.

Can't get a grip and I feel so sick, as I watch it then hit the floor.
The Devil makes a wish, and I'm awaiting that perfect kiss.
Still now today I am being haunted by that number in my head
I just can not find a grip, so I guess this is it.
Time now to finish this story once again....

It Doesn't Add Up

Say today can not we reach it.
The sweet little voice that guides my heart.
The Devil laughs and then he whispers.
His little secret into my hands...

It doesn't add up, the truths that we hide.
It just doesn't add up, the fact you wish not to believe in...

216

Eating the Rainbow

The acid rains deeper into my open flesh.
The wound it is gaping, on the side of my head.
The hours they are falling off of the clock's face.
Then I eat the neon light, the rainbow on my grave.

The mushroom it speaks its opinions.
The unborn child now asks "but why…"
There is such a sinister feeling.
Now it is burning in me.

The acid it seeps deeper into the open flesh.
The now gaping wound on the side of my head.
All the hours are dying and never coming back.
Then I eat the glowing rainbow, shining upon my death.

Neon Blood-Drops

Washed out at the last perverted thought of "Yes".
Then like an earthquake all becomes so very distorted.
Then all the screaming becomes numb and I can only smile.
I laugh and laugh as now this is the end.

The neon blood-drops, they are seeping into the dirt.
Painting the world so beautiful, such elaborate glowing lights.
Then like a monster, I just begin to destroy it.
I truly never meant for this situation to become so awkward.

Washed out in the gutter, that is where I lay waiting for faith.
Come on now God and take me, far passed my world of fear.
Into the depths of all my endless demented rage.
The neon blood-drops taste so sweet, yet cause such an ache.

Fantasy

I feel so frozen to the walls of my mind.
I feel so pasted and out of place at this time.
I know I am wasted and dancing upon another rant.
It is all just a fantasy I live out day after day.

I think that you were mad at me.
For not saying that I will always be there for you.
I just couldn't bring myself to see the top of the hill.
And there I lie, so comfortable in my grave.

Pressing Against

I can see now their faces pressing through the screen.
I want to wake up and admit this is all a dream.
But the ghosts are still moaning long through the night.
And all of the questions are dripping, from off the edge of the knife.

And we cannot just fake it, and say that it makes a little sense.
We must now push forward and leave today gone.
For we need now today, only to leave a little guidance.
As currently the lights are off and we are away...

Society Collapses

Our world it is over, so let us weep.
Our lives they are forgotten, by even you and me.
Our hatred it is flowing, out and into the pit.
So now that we are gone, will we ever be missed?

Our world it is burning, all alone here in space.
Our God he has answered, that one prayer you did ask.
For today shall not the child be vanished?
Our world it is over so let us now together weep.

Join In the Battle

Join in the battle and let us end these wars of the mind.
Join in the struggle and God it is growing cold.
Enjoy the movement of the little insects.
Crawling all through my brain.

Join in the battle and let us complete these wars we wage.
Join in the struggle and admit to all your shames.
Take and tear back at the flesh now.
The only true fear now lost in time...

You Said I Was Real

You said I was real and was such a notion greater.
You said I was alive yet someday will die.
You said that you once loved me.
It is so sad that those years have been erased from my head.

You said I was an angel and could be much more.
You said that I was a dreamer and I am but a bore.
For I am not the demon that is waiting to take control.
You said I was real, and that I should never let go.

Awake In a Seed

Leave us hoping that we might gain the way.
Leave us thinking that we just might be saved.
Leave us to our hoping that tomorrow might shine.
Leave us alone and far behind the line.

I'm now weeping, awake in a seed.
Then I want to escape this, the Devil eating at me.
And God asks for seconds, because he likes the taste.
I am now awake in this seed, growing on only insanity and hate.

Mangled Blisters

Mangled blisters torn at the bottoms of my feet.
For I have been marching onward for just under a decade.
Then all together the shadows hold me from being myself.
I will make it out this time, I will make a stand.

With knees torn and gashed open, blood all over the ground.
So I kneel deep onto the broken glass, and Oh what a laugh.
Left raped and beaten, I am a frightened child all alone.
I just want mommy to save me, but now torn away…

Mangled blisters growing, all bringing on the pain.
For I have not stopped marching, for so many years.
Then I hit a brick wall and at once it was torn down.
For I will make it out this time, no matter the pain.
"I shall stand."

Lethargic Notions

Exhausted philosophy upon this poets tongue.
As then into the nightmare we are all buried alive.
And I was once a better man whom was there.
"I was the one that loved you, I was the one that cared."

I can't bear all of this torment.
Fuck this pointless misled flock of suicidal sheep.
I have tried to save our world once.
But then I sadly died and failed.

Lethargic notions weeping upon my lover's grave.
She would be so happy to know, that we all reached the end.
Now there is only time for one late shot at the rights.
But we cannot reach, then we fall and all is dulled down.
Tripping so far beyond the night.

This Knight Can't Delay

This knight cannot delay, for I shall soon arrive at my home.
This knight can no longer delay, for now the sun will soon set.
This war is so very far from over, it has just now begun.
This pain will not dissipate until I fulfill my vow I've made.
I am coming home my dear to rest so comforted in your arms.
I shall soon return to our beautiful place on top a hill beneath a tall tree.

This knight cannot delay, for the road is still very long indeed.
This knight marches on and will soon be at ease.
For this war shall never be over, it is the evil of the human soul.
"I will return home my dear," to rest safely in your arms.
For I am coming back, and I shall win this war once again.
This knight can't delay, "for I am coming home to you my love..."

Uncompromised

I am for some reason burning myself.
Putting a cigarette out on the back of my hand.
I am gently cutting myself.
There across my wrist.

I am feeling a little uneasy right now.
Maybe because you are a ghost.
I feel so very strange, and then I fade with all the smoke.
Into that place that cannot be...

I am uncompromised here at this chapter.
I am just proving that I was always insane.
I will complete this story, before I'm erased again.

Her Splendid Smiles

Taken back once more upon that road of leaves.
It is a legend that stands true in the eyes of the lost.
Her splendid smiles, they always remind me of then.
A time when we were forgotten, as we are now once again.

Her splendid smiles were always what I needed.
To get me through the day without freaking out!
It was her joyful laughter, that gave me hope sometimes.
It is now at this moment, for you to hit the lights.

Then rushing back to that torment that bleeds from the root.
Taken deep into an artery, pumping back into rage.
It was her laughter that made me once love her.
It was her splendid smiles, which kept all of the evils away.
"But sadly she is gone…"

The Tender Meat

I love the taste of the tender meat.
As it's pulled gently off of the bone.
I love it when you try not to scream.
Because you are afraid that I might hear.

I love it when you try to run.
Then you trip over your own feet.
I love the terror in your eyes.
As you stare up and see me.

I love the taste of the tender meat.
As it's cooked and pulled gently off the bone.
I love it how you try to hide.
But I have found you my love.
I have found you.
I found you…
"Now run!"

222

She Was But a Dream

She was but a dream, echoing on within my head.
She was but a nightmare, the love that I once killed.
She was so great then, but now I know she didn't exist.
She is but a dream, echoing still within my heart.

I was a nothing and still I am to this very day.
I was but a chalked outline, washed away with the rain.
For I wanted but to show you just how to escape hell.
Then I opened my eyes *and I see now that I am falling...*

She was but a dream, from which I wish now to awake.
She was my one true nightmare, my one lingering mistake.
She was such a great friend once, and so was I.
But we are now but dreams, just echoing through out time.

Impressive

If I finished this now would you think it impressive?
If I killed myself would you say you'd be surprised?
If I loaded the gun would you then pull the trigger?
If I begged you would you then cut open my eyes?!

Just bleed out all of what ever it is I have seen.
Tell me that I'm impressive and might some day awake.
Tell me that I was a real poet and not just a fake.
Please remember me my dear, and I am no more...

If I finished this now would you think it to be impressive?
If I killed myself would you ever know that I am gone?
If I loaded the gun and then asked you to pull the trigger.
Would you please just kill me and let me pass away?!.

Chapter 13

On-Top a Hill - Beneath a Tall Tree.

Nonentity

As once my reflection was frittered away.
God had forsaken me and I had lost my name.
I was cast out in the shadow and then became a myth.
I am the nonentity which shall never be missed.

I was once then the creature that lived upon lust.
I was a demon and I destroyed all of her dreams.
I am now just a nothing that amounts to not a thing.
I am the nonentity which shall always and forever be.

As once led into the panic of "I know what I saw!"
Goddamn the fact which I cannot erase from my mind.
I was once then the monster hidden behind your eyes.
I am now the nonentity, forever despised.

The Tide That Beckons

The end is rising and the sun is gone.
The tide it beckons, so time to return home.
The Devil is singing and we need to respond.
All then it slips and into the dire end.

The answers have been questioned.
All of our lives we tried to just be there.
The tide it now beckons, for us to return.
Here now at the end of this new paradigm.

The meanings have been forgotten.
As have all the thoughts of her grace.
It is a residual picture, which needs now to fade.
The end it is calling, so we recede with the tide.

Taste of a Clove

I am so very tired, as if I haven't slept for ages.
I just want to retire, and let my mind rest.
I want to just breathe in, and then exhale all the pain.
I want to rest my eyes, before I fade away.

I can remember how it tastes, such a bitter sweet.
I can remember how it felt, as it dug within me.
I can't be your hero, no not today.
And after all of these years, I can still remember the taste.

I am so very tired, as if I never slept in my life.
I just want to let it all go and just say we'll be alright.
I want now to be at the ending, of what has yet to begin.
I want to reach the next page, and then rest my eyes.

I can remember how it tasted, when she kissed my lips.
I remember how it felt, when we held each other so close.
I remember how it tasted, so cool burning upon my tongue.
And after all of this time, I still can't forget that taste...

She Cradles Me For Ages

It was so great, to be cradled in her arms for ages.
It was so sweet, and she kissed the tip of my tongue.
I need now to forget this, and just wash clean my thoughts.
It was so great, when that night you threw me away.

It was so much darker, when I didn't want to open my eyes.
Here now falling down an endless pit, still I question why.
Have I not been there, to touch the finger tip of the Lord.
I do now see, that hidden truth which is no more.

She held me so close back then, when we were both alive.
She was all that I had ever wanted, that is why I think it was a lie.
I need now to admit it, that I have failed and this is a dream.
Still she cradles me for ages, there in my heart forever unseen.

Never Felt So Dead

I can not just let go.
I will not fail myself.
I must save you, the child.
Which now wanders alone in hell.

I never felt so dead.
Then I break open my tired eyes.
My body it is failing.
But that will not stop me this time.

All my life I have been dreaming.
Yet never have I slept.
All my life I have been dying.
And again I know I am dead.

I can not just let go.
I must save you now my dear.
I will never let go.
Although I've never felt so dead...

Should I Care More?

Should I care more or should I care less?
Could you now tear inside and take what is left.
Yes I do want to just scream now, at the demon in the mirror.
But he just laughs because we are so generally fucked.

Should I be there to watch you give birth to our end.
Should I care more, or just walk away from your sins.
Can I be forgiven, for not correctly using my time?
I am fighting now, to just keep my body upright.

So should I be there to watch our mother-earth being raped?
Should I just scream out all my madness, before it's too late?
Yes I do want this to be over, but at what dire cost.
Should I care more at this moment, or shall I leave you lost?

Schoolyard Memories

Come then and push me onto the ground.
Rub salt in my wounds and watch as I cry.
I am just a child, cast out for I am a little strange.
Come then and push me, into becoming this monster.

Laugh now at the weak little child.
Crying so frantic for all have now cast me out.
Slap me in the face then my friend and say I am a waste.
Come and kill me if you can, and hope I don't get away.

Come then and prove that I am just a child.
Weeping so frantic, because I cannot find my "Mother"...
I am so afraid now, because all has gone so dark.
God take from me these schoolyard memories.
Let me be now but only another forgotten poet.

Skull In the Door

Before you slip back into imaginings.
Smoke dancing about upon the eyes.
All has become so very distorted.
Then the ghost weeps ashes from its eyes.

For I do see the image looming.
Such a detailed skull in the door.
Wood grain yet it is growing.
The haunting image that we all see.

Before you slip back into your dreams of faith.
Know now that the phantoms together sing.
With a blade seeping into the dark.
Just lingering screams, from the skull in the door...

The Ghosts Are Restless

The hopes of gaining are but only dreams.
The thought of failing is more than it seems.
No I cannot just stand this, the pain left within.
Broken shards of lunacy all scattered about.

The ghosts are restless as so am I.
The Devil is gone now and hell is wide open.
We are all at the beginning wanting to see the credits.
This is now our judgment and we are damned.

For one last chance to ever set some logic.
I have been awaiting this so for many ages.
All of the feasting on the bastard's brain, so very sweet.
We are drunk now and poisoned, growing so weak.

The hopes of ever gaining are now only ash.
The thoughts of when I knew it was love, have sadly passed.
No I cannot just deny it, the one last lingering lesson.
For God has spoken and now the ghosts are restless.

I Promised

I promised that I would be there no matter what the cost.
I knew that I was lying and you wouldn't really care.
I never thought that I would never see you again.
So as of now, what can I say?

I promised that I would finish, this story that we started.
I promised that I would truly, give it all my best.
I feel at times that I have failed you, and your memory I have shamed.
I promise that I'll try much harder, to reach the heights peaks.

I tried to say I love you, but it was just too hard that day.
I wanted but only to hold you and let my pains drift away.
I promised that I would save you, but I arrived a moment too late.
I promise now that I will make up, for every mistake I have made.
"Forgive me my love…"

The Day Will Come...

The day will come.
When we will take each other's hand and step over the ledge.
The day will come.
When we are all ready to repent and be judged.
The end must have passed us.
So that would explain why today we are all but frozen ash.
The end must have passed us.
It is so sad to think that we can never again come back.

The day will come.
When we hold each other so close as together we fall.
The day will come.
When we open our eyes to see that all has been lost.
The end must have passed us.
And today we are left standing so silent in shame.
The end must have passed us.
So take my hand and together we step away.

"When We Accept"

When we accept responsibility.
Maybe then we will hold both honor and pride.
I wonder what has gotten into me.
Maybe a lonely demon from hell.

When we accept responsibility.
Then maybe we could both reach the light.
I wonder if, there is a better way for me to go.
When we accept the truth, then we can all let go.

When we accept responsibility.
For completing this war and ending the pain.
I wonder if we'll ever get out of here.
This frozen hell that we both made.

Superstitions

Please don't speak it.
It just might bring bad luck.
Please don't break it.
Seven years then gone to shit.

Please don't speak it.
It just might bring bad luck.
Please be quiet as you dream.
For the walls have ears indeed.

We are so superstitious.
Screaming in dread as the salt is spilt.
We are so superstitious.
Knocking on wood, but we won't ever be saved.

Into Blue Eyes

Into blue eyes, I'm drowning in tears over my head.
Into the ending of a notion, and now I feel so spent.
Jaw locked and I cannot break it.
Into and far beyond the nonsense, we go dancing once again.

Into blue eyes, that is where the end of the riddle rests.
Into the middle of my heart, is now placed that jagged rusted key.
My mind is shaking, body breaking below the stress.
Into and so far beyond, this world that never made any sense.

Into my darkest nightmare, I see now the demon from hell.
He is wearing my face now, and I cannot deny that fact.
And there rests the bloody ax, stuck deep in her head.
From those blue eyes, bleeds out the horror.
The grim fact that now rests beneath the snow.

Constant Gibberish

Of not now breaking.
Metal grinding against teeth.
Against a brick wall beating.
There goes all my brains.
For fucked now like always.
Hammering the needle into the spine.
A tickle upon the edge of reality.
Insanity blooms and we are alive.
Constant gibberish spoken.
Hidden behind the page.
Like a monster that was waiting.
Now seizing the day.
Of right now hated.
Metal against teeth.
Then again the trip is over.
The constant gibberish.
I will forever believe.

The Catalyst

Oh such a twisted method.
As cutting the flesh off of her face.
Oh such blissful pleasure.
As I sew it over my own.

Grip firm the catalyst.
As the earthworms now flood this basement.
Speak verses of the bible.
For the truth is, it shall remain unseen.

Oh such a twisted method.
As cutting out my human soul.
Oh such a blissful pleasure.
Then left bleeding in the cold.

Speak now for no better reasons.
Take now and never give back.
Conclude all that was once divine.
Hold on tight to the catalyst, and we are all now the same.

With the Razor

It was with a razor she opened up her wrist.
It was a very cold winter.
And for a hundred years it did snow.
Lost gone in this place forever.
That which you do not know.

It was with a razor that I began to question this game.
It was so very cold that night.
For one hundred years more it did snow.
Lost gone and hated forever.
And it was with that razor, we shall end this tome.

Bottom Of the Wick

And there it lays waiting at the bottom of the wick.
Twisted beyond all shadows and yes we are all sick.
Into a deeper grave now, head first I fall away.
Six feet away from life, a lifetime away from faith.

And there you lie waiting with cold tears in your eyes.
There you stand weeping, at the cemetery gates.
Into much deeper of now, we all know this is it.
Growing darker and very cold, *"so I'll meet you at the bottom of the wick."*

Nostalgic

I have reached into the heavens.
I have brought back only loss.
I have drunk from the hourglass.
And now all time has slipped away.

I have tried to say that I love you.
I can lie to you but not to myself.
I don't know what it is that I feel at this time.
But if I were to have to guess.
I would say maybe hate.

Salvation Fades

Salvation fades and goes away.
I truly will not be saved this night.
Damnation grows and speaks my name.
So maybe I never was really alive.

Salvation fades and I leave in shame.
I truly wish now to just fucking die.
Damnation comes and takes my hand.
Then we realize what's on the other side.

Salvation fades and I think I am sick.
I want this now to just fucking end.
Come take my hand and lead me away.
Deeper into damnation where all salvation fades.

Jealous...

So that is the truth.
You were just a jealous bitch.
So that's the game.
Endless mounds of poetic lies.

Come take it then and fritter it away.
All is over now and left in the grave.
You were a jealous bitch and thought that you deserved it.
You are dead now, and I don't care anymore.

Searching In the Dark

Forever I have been searching in the dark.
I am so very tormented and sadly torn apart.
I am the missing piece, of the puzzle in your head.
I will always be the darkness beyond the light.
You have always been the thing unable to find.
Forever I have been searching, lost in the dark.
Someday I might find myself.
Here where I have been waiting all this time.

Standing Next to Me

I can smell her perfume, lingering in the air.
I can still feel the touch of her lips against mine.
I can still feel the heartache of so very far passed.
I can still see the outline of her, standing next to me.

I take then a deep breathe and laugh as I'm loading the gun.
I swing all about inside my head, still coming undone.
She was a greater reason, a muse that is now dead.
She might have never existed, but I choose my point of view instead.

I can still smell her perfume, as it lingers in the air.
I can still taste the poison, as it seeps within my flesh.
I want just to hold her, to set my soul free.
But here I wait alone in hell, *"with the memory of her standing next to me."*

Crown of Thorns

Place then this crown of thorns onto my head.
Nail me upside down on a cross again.
Burn me the heretic, for I am a heartless demon.
Raise me up on your mantle, for I am now your God.

Hate me forever and always, "yes" I am talking to you...
Rape me deep within my heart once again.
And yes I think I just reminded myself of our youth.
A fucked up truth, we try to forever hide.

Place then this crown of thorns onto my head.
Judge me now and condemned me to hell.
Burn me and all of my ashes.
Pray to me now, for I am your God.

This Canvas of Flesh

Paint with your blade onto this canvas of flesh.
Make no mistake, for this is our true hell.
Gone and it is waiting, trying to reach an end.
And I live forever as a beautiful art work.
I am forever a painting of both pain and sin.

Push now onto me all of your lies.
Make no mistake, for I shall find you soon.
Gone and you will not expect it, the answer found today.
Now paint much more violent onto this canvas of flesh.
And I will be forever, painted inside of your head.

A Match Half-Burnt

A match half burnt, a life half lived.
A death half found, a life of futile sins.
A match half burnt, as a wrist now shifts.
A love half loved, a beginning upon an ends.

A match half burnt, now surrounded in flame.
Fingernails grinding into my arm, "yes I see you there."
A day half lived, a world half whole.
A match half burnt, symbolic as our souls...
"So please understand."

It Flows Beneath

It rattles around loose in my head.
Mother was lost and never found her way again.
The stars they all fall from every night sky.
The ending it calls, and now it is time.

It all flows beneath, there under my bed.
It all screams so sound somewhere in my head.
It all was a truth that our world did deny.
And all bleeds the tears, from every child's eyes.

In the Flames We Smile

At the bottom of the barrel, hides the secret object.
At the end of the tunnel, here comes a burning freight train.
For miles we have ventured, far out in space.
For so many times now, we have all gone insane.

For the truth of this moment, I am but a tease.
I am truly the poet, infested with a poetic disease.
I have died so many times, just to prove I can.
In the flames now we smile, flowing upon another rant.

At what time "should I end this?" We need not say today.
For so many lives have been spent, all so very grave...
As so many miles we have ventured, far out in the unknown.
In the flames now we smile, admitting we are home.

When I Was Really Me

Can you remember the time, when I caught you before you fell?
Can you remember all the lyrics, of that song that we sang?
Can ever you find it within you, to forgive this tattered soul?
Can please we just end this, before it gets too cold?

I am now the last chance, the pill you must ingest.
Smile as all is now burning, and try not to close your eyes.
See deep into the corruption, this is now Armageddon.
Hold onto me my love, and never let go.

Can you remember a time, when I was really me?
Can you remember the lyrics, of the song that I did sing?
Can ever we be forgiven, for taking that last step?
All now is over, and beginning once again.

Falling Out of Bed

There I go once more.
Falling out of bed.
Into an ocean of boiling tar.
A burning desert of bloody sand.
It is this dying wish now that echoes through time.

We are all dead now.
Just waiting to depart.
It was but only an idea.
It grew into a raging war.
I am falling out of bed again.
And then I smash my head against the floor.

Divine Tongues

Divine tongues are speaking.
Hammering inside my brain.
This world is beginning all the same.
Our minds they are dying, all over again.

The hatred it is flowing.
Flooding my tired mind.
My heart it is bleeding.
Now running out of time.

Divine tongues are screaming.
And I want to save my soul.
Then into the pointless tripping.
Within the endless void.

The hatred it is breaking.
Out of my troubled mind.
My heart it is dead now.
And we are out of time.

The Place I Call Home...

Here I am, back at this place I call home.
There I fall bleeding, and I am all alone.
Mother she is weeping, and wanting me to live.
Here I am back home once more.
To live out all the sins.

Here I go ranting over the death of my heart.
There I fall weeping, pointing out all the scars.
For now we are loving, the feel of going insane.
And now we need only to laugh.
To erase all the pain.

Answer Your Lord

Answer your lord, for he is speaking.
Wipe off your face, for you are bleeding.
Take care of your life now, for it is coming to an end.
Turn off the lights now, and let the games begin.

Answer all the nonsense, for now it is time.
Follow on in this riddle, hidden within the limes.
Take back all the torment, that once made me – me.
Answer your Lord, for now he sadly bleeds.

Rolling the Pill

There I go, rolling the pills down my throat.
There we are laughing, at all our mistakes.
There all the pain it is writhing, behind the glowing moon.
There I go beating, the nonsense far beyond noon.

So there we go screaming, rolling the pills down our throats.
There we are dying, as we all begin to choke.
There was once a point then, now only our mistakes.
As swallowing all the pills, to ease all the pain.

The Zombie Dreams

It is cooler out now, winter growing strong.
It is darker at this time, six feet below.
It was a wish that the weeping child made.
To be saved from all the pain and the shame.

This zombie is now moaning, waking to seek revenge.
It is the wish of the child, for me to return and feed.
All of the child's enemies will soon fall and be at my feast.
This zombie wants to be there, to satisfy the child's dreams.

It is cooler out tonight, in the grave where I stand.
It is darker this night, and now this zombie will rise.
To fulfill all the child's dreams and ease all the pain.
This zombie is now ready, to take control of this torment...

Fucking Hypocrites

Fuck your bullshit and all that you say.
Fuck all the voices that infest your retarded brain.
Fuck all the lies of your hypocritical world.
Just shut your fucking mouth and maybe you will learn.

Goddamn all the bitterness that is your shallow faith.
Damn all your nonsense that is bleeding from your head.
Fuck all the hypocrites, I wish they'd all just die.
Fuck you and your beliefs, all so jaded and dim.

Yes fuck all the pointlessness of your thoughts.
Get out of my way and shut the fuck up!
Goddamn this torment, of "you" I must endure.
Damn all the fucking hypocrites, which plagues our dying world.

The Dirt Feels Cooler

The dirt feels cooler as I awake below.
This mind has been shattered and left all alone.
This world has just ended and no one did see.
As I kissed the lips of God and admitted insanity.

Yes the dirt it feels cooler as I wake all alone.
This mind has just drifted, deep below the waves.
This world it just ended and no one did see.
As I smiled and let it all just fade.

Cradle of Leaves

There I sleep upon a cradle of leaves.
There I die and just fade away.
Yes I am happy that we all have seen the end.
Again we are leading, deep into the abyss.

Come follow me down into the darkest truth.
Love me no matter what the cost.
And you know that I will forever love you.
Come wake me now so I can see it all start.
As I lie here cold, upon a cradle of leaves.

Resting My Mind

I am now resting my mind, so very tranquil.
I have reached into the open heart of God.
Then I became but a dream.

I am now resting my mind.
Ready for another day.
I have become but a bore.
So now my love, just turn the page…

"So laugh with us for we have reached the end."

The Perfect Kiss

So very calm now, resting on top a hill beneath a tall tree.
I can remember the feel, of when she once held me.
It was so very great then, the times when we were together.
So very great, when all felt as but a dream.

Then at once we had reached an ending.
But it was all so blissful as she told me to let go.
I can remember just what it was like, to be so at peace.
It was so very great then, all the times when we just laughed.

I begin to wonder, what if I had held on a bit more.
Just to say *I love you*, "*as she had waited up all night.*"
I begin to wonder, what if I had stayed instead...
But then I remember, what she had once said.

So very calm now, resting on top a hill beneath a tall tree.
I can remember the feeling, of when she said I was real.
It was all so very great back then, *and now I can remember what we said.*
Out of all in my existence, I cherish most – that perfect kiss...

"*When we had said goodbye...*"

Extras:

Wars of the Mind Vol.1 (Upon the Road of Leaves.) was written between the years 2001 and 2005 and follows through the beginnings of young poet/vocalist Jonathan W. Haubert's career in music and writing. Sharing in many personal details of Jonathan and his bandmates. Upon the Road of Leaves is a rough and grim path which leads the young poet and his fellow bandmates through many years of pain, hope, fear, loss, joy and death. Wars of the Mind Vol.2 (Beneath a Frozen Lake.) was written between the years 2005 and 2006. Volume 2 follows immediately after the conclusion of Volume 1, when Jonathan had found himself at the brink of a nervous/mental break-down after suffering the unexpected loss of his grandfather, the end of a four year long relationship with his girlfriend, and the suffering of the band all going their separate ways after only a few short years of live shows while writing "Upon the Road of Leaves." During the writing of "Beneath a Frozen Lake." Jonathan found himself in a constant state of inebriation due to his growing depression until - through the music and poetry - Jonathan found the inner strength to overcome his ongoing battles with depression, drugs and alcohol. In the conclusion of "Beneath a Frozen Lake." Jonathan was able to find sobriety and a small glimpse of hope beyond the endless madness. In the beginnings of Wars of the Mind Vol.3 (Behind Open Doors.) - written between the years 2007 and 2008 - this third chapter in the Wars of the Mind series was a new evolution in Jonathan's mental, spiritual and emotional battles. Volume 3 (Behind Open Doors.) paves the way for a new chapter in the music and poetry of Wars of the Mind and follows the adventures of Jonathan into the studio with his solo project titled EuQiNu in the recording of four original albums...
Wars of the Mind Vol.4 (On-Top a Hill – Beneath a Tall Tree.) - written between the years 2009 and 2010 - follows Jonathan through both relapse and triumph. Jonathan fell back into the use of drugs and alcohol to help calm his intense mental and emotional battles until a twist of fate led to the reuniting of Jonathan W. Haubert and Julio C. Salazar in the reformation of COUNT YOUR DEAD. Now back writing music with long-time friend and guitarist Julio, through stage, studio and endless amounts of hours put into writing and rehearsal, Jonathan was able to find the inner strength to overcome and prevail leading to the release of Count Your Dead's debut album "NO RETURN" and the writing of Wars of the Mind Vol.5 (Between Flesh & Bone.)

Thanks:

I would like to thank my family and friends for always being there for me.
And all my brothers in music and the fans, thank you all for helping me through all the good and bad times. And I would like to once more thank you the reader.
For taking this 4th journey into the Wars of the Mind.
And to everyone who picks up this book.
And holds it true to their heart. "I thank you all."

www.countyourdead.com

Tear the bones out, *then what is left in me?*
Take the pain out, *and what is left of me?*
Tear your heart out, *then just watch it bleed!*
Take the hate out, *and what is left of me...?*
"Say when."

(Jonathan W. Haubert)

Coming Soon:

Wars of the Mind
Vol. 5: (*Between Flesh & Bone.*)